Revolutionary
Marriage

Revolutionary Marriage

How to Have a Marriage
that Changes the World

Dr. Mark DeYoung, LMFT

Revolutionary Marriage
How to Have a Marriage that Changes the World

Published by: DeYoung Consulting, Inc.

ISBN: 978-0-9911311-8-1
ISBN: 978-0-9911311-9-8 (eBook)

Printed in the United States of America.

Dedication

To my wife, Patricia
Sharing life with you gives me glimpses of Jesus
You love deeply and sacrifice for our family
Your example is my best teacher for marriage
I am a better man because of you

Table of Contents

Endorsements

I have known Dr. Mark DeYoung for many years. I know his passion for healing hurting and broken relationships. As a longtime board member for Christ's Haven for Children, a widely respected not-for-profit organization that serves children, I have witnessed his work in action. He developed tools for measuring the progress of the children in the care of Christ's Haven and the effectiveness of its various programs.

In this book, Dr. DeYoung identifies flawed cultural ideas about marriage, seeks to identify the higher purposes of marriage, and redefines a successful marriage. His advice finds its roots in scholarly studies, biblical wisdom, and thousands of hours of marital counseling. His revolutionary approach could reverse the tragic story of marriages afflicted by the ailments of a broken world. His thinking gives a proven and practical path for married partners to walk together in the peace and joy of Christ.

I heartily recommend Dr. DeYoung's book to anyone who seeks a healthier marriage.

Joe Tolbert
Attorney, board member Christ's Haven for Children

Marriage books are a dime a dozen. Who needs another one?

We all do; society needs this crucial book by Dr. Mark DeYoung!

This book tells the hard truth and doesn't offer a retread of quick fix tools which have not produced meaningful change. DeYoung's *Revolutionary Marriage* is a welcome and essential tool that calls us to embrace a radical approach to marriage. It also offers understandable and doable steps toward establishing healthy marriages amid an individualistic culture that is highly toxic to marriage. Mark writes from a depth of understanding, but makes the principles and practices for building a healthy marriage simple to understand without being simplistic or idealistic. I love his approach to "supplementarian" marriage and talk of marriage as vocation. Yes, you need to read *Revolutionary Marriage*. But you also need a supply you can give to others."

Dr. Dan Bouchelle
President, Mission Resource Network

An inspiring book which will propel you and your spouse to a new level of unity and spiritual maturity. Dr. DeYoung presents concepts which are therapeutically sound and highly effective in building success in a Christian marriage relationship, benefiting your entire family. A must read for anyone wanting to solidify their marriage and influence future generations.

Tina Johnston,
Psychotherapist, Director of NewStarts
www.CreateNewStarts.com

Mark DeYoung's *Revolutionary Marriage* is one of the top marriage books that I have read. In a clear style that is deeply theological, practical, and relevant, Mark offers us a captivating vision of marriage. With honesty and realism, he explains why marriage has fallen into such disrepair. But, he also explains how we can rescue it. I wish I could have grasped these principles earlier in my own marriage. I will certainly be passing this book on to others. I'll also share these concepts, to my congregation, my children, and to all who desire a richer and broader picture of what a Christian marriage can be.

I found the content of this book intellectually stimulating, emotionally convicting, and spiritually challenging. In other words, this book made me think and cry and pray. Thanks, Mark, for giving us a grand picture of what marriage can be!

Steve McMillan
Lead Pastor, Bow Valley Community
Church, Calgary Canada

Revolutionary Marriage changes the conversation on marriage!

Mark DeYoung tears down the infrastructure of the antiquated ideology of marriage and the methodology of marital counseling. He then rebuilds it on God's original foundation for marriage. But he also followed architecture that arches over postmodern skepticism, social constructs, and division within the Church. If marriage is in your past, present, or future, this is a resource you should have!

Ryan Young
Christian Minister,
Former NFL Athlete, and Husband

Revolutionary Marriage is a trusted tool on my bookshelf and a recommended reading to my students. Why? Mark does an excellent job framing marriage in the category of vocation and removes it from the romanticized, self-actualization pinnacle often framed by religious and contemporary cultures. Dr. DeYoung avoids the "quick fix" temptation taken by many and provides a practical "So What's Next" pathway for marriages. Thank God, somebody believes marriage can survive and thrive amidst the various challenges presented in today's contemporary culture.

Mark is my friend and trusted advisor. I am so proud of his work on this project. I love his passion for helping couples thrive in their marriage and for assisting those who work with couples. I highly recommend *Revolutionary Marriage* to my married friends, those thinking about marriage, and to my pastor, professor and counseling colleagues.

Dr. David Fraze
Assistant Professor, Endowed Chair Youth and Family
Ministry Program, Lubbock Christian University

Acknowledgments

*F*irst, I thank the following individuals for reading and providing valuable feedback on this book. Mike and Linda Bell, Patricia DeYoung, Joe Tolbert, David Fraze, Steve McMillan, Dan Bouchelle, Tina Johnston, Elizabeth Carlson, Dudley and Martha Harris, Andy and Kia Bondurant, and Ryan Young.

I thank my daughters, Rayna and Rebekah. You girls continually bless me and your mom. Your decisions to honor us as your parents do not go unnoticed.

I thank all the couples that have invited me into their homes and marriages to work towards healthier relationships. You have taught me much.

I feel lucky to call Ed Chinn friend. Though distant by miles, when we talk it is like we pick up a conversation from yesterday. I cannot measure my appreciation for your editing help. You have always been an encourager to me.

Thank you, Gene Villarreal, for your photographic work and your attention to detail.

Disclaimer:
All names and identifying details have been changed to protect the privacy of individuals. Stories of couples have been fictionalized to protect their identity.

Preface

*I*t is the story of dreams. A young couple. In love. Making plans for a wedding. Their friends celebrate their delightful and beautiful relationship. A spirit of innocent vulnerability unites them. There are late-night parties where dreams are shared around laughter and food. The engagement story is a fairy tale. He planned it for a month and enlisted the help of close friends. It involved dinner at one of their favorite spots and a candlelit proposal under the stars. The photos and videos illustrate their love story. They attend church regularly. Resisting cultural norms, they have chosen to remain sexually pure before their wedding night. Because they share a deep faith, they believe their future will be blessed and protected from the pains they have seen with others. Premarital counseling has increased their resolve and faith to live out a perfect match. Their faith in God, assurance in their relationship, and their maturity have laid a solid foundation for a growing intimacy. If you were to talk with them, you would share their confidence and joy that they are on the right track.

Most Christian marriages begin with emotional vulnerability, shared vows, and energetic vitality. Conflicts are easily reconciled, commitment is strongly expressed, and there is a feeling of new life, like springtime. It is part of the bonding process that draws couples together. Though there are marriages that have a rockier start, and you may have a hard time remembering happier moments, there were likely enough of these goods to help establish the marriage. So, regardless of how deep these connections, there is often a nearly universal feeling of optimism at the beginning of any marriage.

The wedding day comes and goes. The pictures of the event are in the album. The honeymoon is over, and social media "likes" are a brief flurry of validation. This couple must be bound for bliss. Except—life happens.

I have seen many of these marriages in my counseling practice. They are the couple who...

- have never found a satisfying sexual rhythm that is mutually enjoyable.
- are so far in debt they don't know where the next house payment is coming from.
- have struggled with alcohol and have even driven the kids to school drunk.
- have filed for divorce, changed their mind, and filed again.
- have secret emotional affairs with coworkers through texting.

Why do marriages experience such pain? What are the causes of so many marriages breaking up? These are questions I have asked during my two decades of work with families, and the answers are complex. I believe marriage as an institution has undergone seismic changes in the last several decades. The role marriage plays in families has moved away from a foundational bedrock to an uncertain and often unpredictable relationship. How we define marriage has become less clear. If you ask Christians why they get married, or what is the purpose of marriage, their answers will illustrate this lack of clarity. I believe Christians have lost a certainty for what marriage is intended to be, and the importance of the true purposes of marriage.

This book is intended to present a revolutionary, countercultural model of marriage, because this is ultimately the Bible's call for marriage. What I propose here will confront both secular and current Christian views of marriage. The task is large, and the work between spouses will be difficult. Because of this, the approach must be radical and the appeal for change between couples significant—rather than just loving each other better or communicating with greater clarity—I propose that couples have a revolutionary task to change the world through the work of living and working out challenges within their marriage. That is the central thesis of this book—marriage serves a purpose greater than the two partners and their personal self-fulfillment.

The reader will find a little bit of theology, some current social science theory, and some solid practical guidance for help with Christian marriages. This book is intended to challenge Christian couples to live out the higher purposes of marriage outlined in scripture. I encourage every reader to apply the truths within the pages, and I am confident it will change the way you love, live, and share life together.

I am often overwhelmed with the enormity of this challenge for the Christian marriage in our culture. As a therapist, I know many books and seminars that offer solutions for broken marriages. And though many of these books have good ideas, I often find them to fall short of pressing Christian marriage towards the revolutionary purposes outlined in scripture. I have grown increasingly restless with my desire to share the ideas in this book. The truths presented here are what I use daily in my therapeutic work with couples. I have great confidence in the ideas I will share, which is why I use them as the support framework for my counsel with couples. I have seen the benefits in the narrow context of couples' therapy, and I want to make the courageous step to challenge more couples in a public forum to higher purposes.

Chapter 1
Revolutionary Marriage

Cassie felt desperate, angry, and hopeless. I listened as her voice moved from tearful sadness to disgust. Her husband, Cory, had been having an affair. It wasn't a one-night stand, but an ongoing relationship of several months. Cassie discovered his text messages this past weekend. Though Cory initially denied it, when the truth became undeniable, he confessed. He said he had ended it and he wanted to stay in his marriage. He expressed remorse. But Cassie was not sure she could trust him. How could she remain with this man who had hurt her so deeply, after 20 years of marriage? How could Cory do this to her and their family? Where did she fail? Where did they fail?

First meetings in marriage therapy dealing with affairs are often tense. Distrust is thick and hope is thin. We met for the first session and processed the depths of their doubts and established some plans for accountability. We wanted to begin by restoring some trust. In future sessions, we faced the details of the affair and processed the rage resulting from such a betrayal. Cory was repentant, but Cassie remained deeply distrustful.

Over several weeks, Cassie struggled with indecision about remaining in the marriage. She explored the consequences and ramifications of divorce for herself and for their children. Cory remained both accountable and repentant. His choice to remain vulnerable began to soften Cassie.

We explored forgiveness and the hard but necessary choice to stop making each other pay for the injuries in the marriage. These were hard discussions; the choice to forgive is risky. Though it might be the right decision, the risk of being injured again often leads husbands and wives to withdraw into a bunker of protection.

I honestly don't have words to explain what happened next with Cassie and Cory (and with other couples I have seen on this journey). We saw a release, a washing, a surrender. Although I have seen it many times in my work with couples, it is always a sweet surprise. Even after years of experience, I can never predict when it will occur. But when this submission (by both partners) occurs, a new space opens up for healing in the marriage. Forgiveness and reconciliation blossomed between them.

I still hear from them every once in a while. They are doing very well. Their marriage remains strong, and the once painful wounds have become scars that bind them closer together.

How does a marriage overcome such trauma? The healing Cory and Cassie experienced can happen with most any couple. The principles presented in this book can help couples discover those healing practices daily. And, when they live out these ideas daily, marriage fulfills its intended purpose. Much like Cory and Cassie modeled reconciliation and grace on a large scale, every marriage is called to that mission daily, on a small scale. This book is a call to radically change your marriage, a call to live out submission rather than to seek satisfaction.

In more than 20 years of working with couples as a Licensed Marriage and Family Therapist, I have come to believe that many Christians in our culture have lost their way with marriage. Many have allowed the romanticism and narcissism of our age to creep into the marriage relationship. That has moved Christian marriage away from their unique purposes, as portrayed in scripture. That gradual change has alarmed and confused many Christians and church leaders.

Here is what I see and hear from both secular and Christian marriages:

When couples try to do "everything right," they are often surprised when they encounter problems and traumas. They wonder how it could get so bad if they did things so right in the beginning. Popular literature and media fill our minds with idealistic notions that marriage with the right person, under the right conditions, can bring utopian bliss. Because of the confusion and ambiguity about marriage in our society, sometimes couples start out living together, to "test the waters." That goes well... until it doesn't. Then, they become surprised that things change dramatically after the wedding. How could things be fine when living together but go so dreadfully wrong after they marry? That question has plagued researchers for decades, and we will explore it later. But, whether you "do everything right" or "test the waters," our culture's influence and experience of marriage take it in the wrong direction.

I have concluded that marriage is not for the wimpy, the immature, or the starry-eyed romantic. Marriage is a full contact sport for grownups. Rather than swallowing an idealistic notion of blissful union, Christian couples need to expect and prepare for real and challenging struggles. The joy in marriage does not come from dreamy romantic experiences (though they can be delightful); it comes from deeply knowing and being deeply known. That "knowing" takes work and is a profoundly spiritual act. That is because our weaknesses are both exposed and nurtured. As a result, we grow toward fulfilling the true purposes of being created in the image of God.

That happened with Cory and Cassie. After experiencing traumas to the intimacy of their relationship, they chose to persist, forgive, and reconcile instead of letting the stress tear them apart. For Christian marriages to be revolutionary at a daily micro-level, they are called to engage in committed, forgiving, and submissive connections.

Marriage in Crisis

The institution and idea of marriage have passed through deep change since the Industrial Revolution, and even more serious challenge since the Sexual Revolution, now over 50 years ago. No other time in human history has seen marriage battered by such dramatic changes. What was long accepted as the foundational relationship for all families is no longer accepted as necessary or even ideal. Marriage has been defined for millennia as a heterosexual, monogamous relationship. But, current trends have shattered the very definition of marriage. And fast. I see four cultural trends—same-sex marriage, marital affairs, cohabitation, and divorce—as the primary reasons for a radical change in perspective and practice in Christian marriages. Each of those trends challenges us to sharpen our focus on the definition of marriage. Adjusting our perspectives can serve the purposes for which God created marriage.

Same-Sex Marriage

Twenty-four nations in the world recognize same-sex marriage. This is a recent phenomenon, with the oldest legal recognition (the Netherlands) going back to 2000 (the United States made it legal in 2015). A 2016 Pew Research poll found that 55% of Americans support same-sex marriage.[1] Though that number has been rising since 2000, it does not tell the complete story. Political ideology shapes how people view the issue. Seventy-eight percent of liberals support it, compared

---

1 Hannah Fingerhut, Support steady for same-sex marriage and acceptance of homosexuality, Pew Research Center, May 12, 2016
https://www.pewresearch.org/fact-tank/2016/05/12/
support-steady-for-same-sex-marriage-and-acceptance-of-homosexuality/.

to 29% of conservatives. Religion also brings significant differences in approval rates. According to the same Pew Research poll, support for same-sex marriage breaks out along the following religious lines:

- White evangelical (27%)
- Black Protestant (39%)
- Catholics (58%)
- White Mainline Protestant (64%)
- Unaffiliated with church (80%)

Although I find no examples of biblical endorsement of same-sex relationships in the Bible, I did not write this book as a statement on same-sex marriages. But, I want to be clear for the reader; when the Bible addresses marriage, it always means heterosexual, monogamous relationships. So, that is the focus of *Revolutionary Marriage*.

This issue has changed the landscape of marriage more than any other in human history. Because same-sex marriage has been driven by dramatic changes in cultural values and is also influenced by many misguided perspectives of marriage (even within churches), we will explore it further in Chapter 3.

Extramarital Affairs—Swinging and Other Forms of Polyamory

Marital affairs have both increased and become more diverse. What used to be the shameful one-night stand or highly secretive relationship has become more brazen and acceptable. Several factors have contributed to the rise in sex outside marriage: American obsession with sex, increased acceptance of diverse sexual behaviors, the internet, social media, more private communication (email, texting, other messaging apps), and increased access to pornography. Swinging clubs (allowing couples to trade sexual partners) are on the rise and easily accessible on the internet. Popular websites promote affairs with married individuals. In "consensual nonmonogamy," an increasing number of people choose "nonromantic" marriages for economic benefits, but openly seek romantic and sexual partners outside their marriage. Many of these behaviors seem to enjoy increased acceptance because "everyone is doing it."

Today, sexual freedom seems to capture a cultural rallying cry in America. Social research often describes sexual affairs as a man's effort to "spread his seed" for evolutionary survival. Researchers also describe female sexual expression as a rebellion against centuries of sexual repression by patriarchal cultures. Those viewpoints of sexual expression are incomplete and often ignore personal responsibility, self-control, and restraint as important factors in sexual expression. But, healthy sexuality must go beyond "meeting needs" to experiencing sex as a gift that includes both grace and submission.

Helping couples dealing with affairs (one-night stands, prostitution, and serial affairs) has been a significant part of my practice, and the frequency of those cases is increasing rapidly. Every situation is unique, and the injuries cut deep. The sexual problems in marriage require a major paradigm shift. Christian marriages should—and must—rise above our culture's view of sex. The Christian marriage approach to sexual intimacy should be antithetical to how it is presented in our culture. Sex is not a need, it is a gift. In Christian marriage, compassion precedes sexual passion, and submissive service replaces selfish satisfaction. Ultimately, the very core of the sexual experience starts with safety. And, safety is built on trust. Self-focus and personal fulfillment damage relationships. We will discuss this more in Chapter 4.

Cohabitation Continues to Rise

Before the 1960s, cohabitation was secretive and only practiced by a few. By 1970, there were approximately 500,000 unmarried couples living together in the United States. That number has risen dramatically through the decades: 1.5 million (1980), 2.9 million (1990), 4.2 million (1998), and 7.8 million (2012). The acceptance of such arrangements has also increased. Rates are higher with lower incomes and lower levels of education. Forty percent of cohabitations transition to legal marriage within three years; increased age and higher levels of education move that percentage up to 50%. Some researchers have proposed that these differences result from age and commitment. It seems couples that are older and have a stated commitment to marry are more likely to find relationship success. The divorce rate among such couples is not any higher than in couples that do not live together before marriage.

Many within Christian circles have condemned, even demonized, cohabitation without always understanding the complex nature of such relationships. Many also idolize legal marriages as if a piece of paper from the local courthouse carries the antidote to broken marriages. Yet, Christian marriages dissolve at rates similar to the rest of the population. The truth behind successful marriage is much more complex and includes qualities such as personal maturity (readiness for marriage) and a publicly stated commitment to the relationship. My work with many cohabiting couples, and many couples that are now legally married, after living together, confirms the research. Legal documentation of a marriage does not cement a relationship. Stability in a marriage is much more connected to maturity and accountability.

Wait. So, how are Christians supposed to protect the importance of marriage? Yes, ceremony and ritual help to establish a marriage. Yet, when we emphasize the need to be legally married (probably too strongly), we miss out on the most important aspects of marriage. We all know couples who got married without being prepared for all that comes with marriage. It is easy to get married, but a huge challenge to stay married. Our emphasis should move beyond the "acts" of marriage to the foundational components of connection and commitment that make marriages stable. We will discuss these ideas more fully in Chapter 5.

Divorce Rates and Changes in Perspective

Divorce rates are complicated and very difficult to calculate. But, the popular belief that 50% of marriages end in divorce is not accurate. In fact, the likelihood of a marriage ending in divorce is currently between 40% and 50%. This number has been declining slightly in the past few years. Still, that is too many divorces. And, that is because it reflects the death of what was once vital and alive.

Many in churches have railed against divorce without seeing or talking about the factors that might contribute to divorce. Despite our "just don't do it" mantra, Christian marriages seem to divorce near the same rate as couples unaffiliated with a church. In my work with couples, I have seen that most Christian definitions of successful marriage have been too limited. We seem to think as long as a couple does not get divorced the marriage is successful. That presents a pitiful and impoverished standard for success. The call on marriage in scripture is much higher, and the standard for success is greater than just sharing the same house. Sharing a residence for 50 years is not an adequate sign of life for a marriage.

Christians must see marriage as a call to higher purposes and standards. Marriage needs to fit into the very work of God on this earth. Marriage is not about self-fulfillment, but about sacrifice to fulfill the greater purposes of God's kingdom. As an author, I want to identify the higher purposes of marriage and redefine what we call a successful marriage. That will help us establish higher goals for marriage. Christ-followers must catch a vision for marriage beyond simply meeting individual needs for love, attention, and sexual fulfillment. A self-oriented focus in marriage only leads to death and decay. But, submission and sacrifice (the true scriptural calls on marriage) reflect the resurrection power of Christ, right here and right now.

We will discuss these ideas more in Chapter 6.

Marriage Defined

As stated earlier, until recently, society saw marriage as a committed heterosexual relationship that encompassed physical and spiritual dimensions. That's why most marriage ceremonies were performed in religious settings. But, that definition and experience are becoming less common. This book is a revolutionary call for the marriage relationship to return to the principles and purposes for which it was created.

Since I based this book on biblical texts, marriage will be defined as follows:

- A heterosexual relationship (Genesis 1:26-28; 2:24)
- A sexually monogamous relationship (Matthew 5:27-28; I Corinthians 6:12-20)
- Marriage requires intentional sexual connection (I Corinthians 7:1-5)
- Sexual, sacred, and spiritual dimensions make marriage unique to any other human relationship (Ephesians 5:32)

This definition should shape our thinking toward creating marriages that reflect God's kingdom. The more we see that, the more it will move us beyond the cultural battles toward a higher calling and purpose for our marriages.

What is "Revolutionary Marriage?"

A revolution is not just something different or new; it's *radical*. So, what separates marriages based on Christian principles from those that are not? Shouldn't there be *some* clear difference?

Sadly, many people in churches and Christian homes just model popular culture. But, those homes and families do not seem better for it. So, what makes marriage "revolutionary"? How can we present a clearer picture of the Christian view of marriage? Shouldn't Christian life differ from the dominant culture? Shouldn't Christian marriage be measured by a higher law?

So, how do we, as individuals and married couples, relate to our culture? Well, to start, Christians should work on listening more and offering fewer directives. Those who are more progressive on social issues need to allow freedom of choice rather than demanding others to move to their "more refined" way of thinking. And, we can all use a little dose of humility. What if we all listen, empathize, and seek to understand rather than demanding that others change?

Beyond that, one reason marriages are suffering an identity and stability crisis is that our culture has blurred the marriage definition. So, what better way to start a revolution than to make the boundary lines very clear?

Before 1960, marriage was an accepted part of the cultural fabric. But, today, we are more diverse and more confused. Our culture has slowly allowed something that was clear to become unclear. In our western world, the participants define marriage. We've lost the objective definitions and measurements. Without a true definition, we have nothing to point to. And, without a means to measure belief and behavior by an eternal plumb line, we have no standard to live by.

Marriage *is* a revolutionary idea. It pulls two unique and flawed adults into an alliance, a relationship, that lasts a lifetime. Imagine, two individuals with such drastic differences—gender, histories, values, strengths, weaknesses, and maturities—daring to share life, solve problems, organize, and raise their children. When we consider all human partnerships, such as neighborhood associations, business agreements, and international treaties, we find failures are common. Those failures may constrain our hopes for marriage.

Yet marriages last. Some of our greatest stories of love, valor, trust, and commitment come from marriages. At their very best, marriages inspire and teach us about higher values and ideals. At their worst, marriages wound and destroy. We've all seen it. What dangerous and exciting territory to explore. What a ripe environment for a revolution.

So, let's forge ahead. Let's look at this radical idea of marriage that is so rich with meaning and value for our lives, our families, and our communities.

We will start with marriage becoming tainted and then explore its sacred ideal.

REGROUP

Full and vigorous conversations help to build intimacy in marriage. I have designed the "So What's Next?" sections at the end of each chapter to help create those intimate exchanges. I hope these will help the readers take the material from the chapter and apply it in deep ways to their marriages.

In this chapter, we have tried to establish that Christian marriages face challenges. That's because marriage is hard work, especially amid cultural pressures. In his research with couples, Dr. John Gottman talks about the value of couples "glorifying the struggle."[2] He says healthy couples can 1) embrace the hardships of marriage as beneficial, and 2) can celebrate their difficulties. I designed the following exercise to help create a "glorifying the struggle" moment.

Purpose

The following exercise should help you regroup and prepare for the journey forward by looking back.

Plan

Make sure you find the right time, place, and emotional temperature for this activity. Don't use this activity to

2 John M. Gottman, Julie Schwartz Gottman, Doug Abrams, and Rachel Carlton Abrams, *Eight Dates: Essential Conversations for a Lifetime of Love.* (New York, Workman Publishing Company, 2018).

address problems. Prepare and expect to connect and better understand each other and your marriage.

Practice

Start with prayer. If you are not in the habit of praying together, this can be a good place and way to start. Jesus said, "Ask." So, *ask* God very specifically to help you see how He has brought your marriage through challenges, how He helped each of you to grow, and how He made your marriage stronger.

1. Each of you shares a challenge that your marriage has passed through. Be careful that you share in gratitude to God, not criticism of your spouse. Whether you both share the same or different events, be sure to explore the events at each point in the steps below.

2. Share how you each felt during the difficult season(s). Be specific. Share actual feelings and words (sad, angry, hurt, scared, disappointed, etc.). Be sure to note how you felt in each of the struggles you identified in step 1.

3. Take turns for each to share the most challenging part of those difficult times. Make sure that each of you reflects what you heard from your partner to ensure they feel understood. Ask, "Do you feel like I understand what was most difficult for you?"

4. Make room for each to share what he and she learned about the other and about the marriage through that struggle. What you present here

should be positive, not critical of the other partner. For example, rather than saying, "I learned you can disappoint me," consider something like, "Though I was disappointed, I learned you can keep your word."

5. Discuss how those past experiences have grown or improved your marriage. Talk about what you have received from that struggle.

6. End with prayer, asking God to take this newly identified strength and use it to grow your marriage.

Chapter 2
Unholy Marriage

*I*t felt like World War III. Every session was loud and chaotic. Tom was loud and profane, and Sue could match his foul language with ferocity. They argued about everything—sex, money, parenting, time together, and even what to eat for dinner. Each session followed the same pattern. Sue would speak a litany of complaints, and Tom would get defensive. The back and forth would escalate until Tom or Sue would storm out of the room and go outside for a smoke.

Each of my interventions fell short; I couldn't stop the expanding arguments. It felt futile; eventually, the therapy with Tom and Sue ended in a fizzle, with no resolution. I don't know if they ever got better. Unfortunately, they were caught in a hopeless cycle of battles.

Working with Tom and Sue helped me see how bad it could get in marriage. It was dark and discouraging. I know many couples have experienced that deep brokenness in marriage. Their marriages have moved from meadows of hope to scorched battlegrounds.

Couples therapy often requires me to manage the back and forth, tit-for-tat disagreements of warring couples. Husband and wife launch verbal assaults and complaints about the other. I have often seen how they both seem to retreat to their individual castles to protect their fragile egos and emotions. From behind those walls, they will fire the most destructive verbal assault into their partner's castle walls. They seem dead set on exposing his or her issues while remaining safe in their own fortifications. Then they increase their protection by building thicker walls of disconnection. They each see success as withstanding all assaults, while breaking down the failings of their spouse. Each seems to believe if their partner's flaws are exposed and fixed, then the marriage would be a happier place. Personal vulnerability is out of the question, disconnection grows, and ultimately intimacy is lost on their battlefield. Wedding vows become mere remnants of a once-beautiful dream, now buried in the rubble of the battle.

How do marriages get to that place? Why isn't marriage as fulfilling as many expected? People spend millions each year on marriage and self-help books that suggest new techniques for improved communication. They are often read by wives, who then place the books conspicuously on their husband's nightstand. Where they collect dust. Both parties keep adding ammunition which they will launch in a later fight. Why are the self-help and communication books not helping? Why are so many Christian marriages seemingly no better than the non-Christian ones?

Many Christians and whole churches buy books that promote male leadership and female submission. Though pulled from the pages of scripture, they often leave men feeling inadequate and confused about how to lead without being domineering. Clearly, the factors contributing to failing Christian marriages are deeper than the solutions offered in many of these self-help books.

In my work with couples over two decades, I've tried to use the best tools and techniques available to help couples reconcile their marriage. I have become increasingly concerned that the failure of many marriages has been because of our myopic cultural view of marriage. I have longed for a deeper, richer view of marriage. And, I want to hear a call from Christians for marriage to be more than we are living out. I believe that could help Christian marriage rise above the cultural fray.

I hope this book will add to and improve that conversation. We need a revolutionary call for marriages to be radically different from our culture's marriage model. Marriage calls us into the mystery and beauty of deeper intimacy and faith with God.

We need to hear:

- Marriage is more about being holy than being whole.
- Marriage requires the death of self rather than self-actualization.
- Marriage brings glory to God by celebrating men and women as unique image-bearers, not glory to your family.

Before we explore these richer and deeper ideas in the next chapter, let's look at how marriage moved away from its sacred nature to become an often-unholy alliance.

The Historical Problem

Marriage, the union of a man and woman in a committed alliance, was God's ideal from the beginning. But right from the start, human selfishness and conflict became part of the marriage relationship. And in a fallen and broken creation, marriage has continued to struggle to fulfill its Creator's purpose. More recently, marriage has absorbed the heavy assaults that have blocked the marital union from being everything that God intended.

The choice Adam and Eve made to eat the fruit brought a curse on themselves and their descendants. God spelled out the natural consequences of choosing the fruit rather than walking with Him in the garden:

1. The first consequence was **damage** or brokenness. Things will not work as intended. Childbirth would become difficult (Genesis 3:16) and the ground would be cursed (Genesis 3:17); it would only produce through hard work. Eve's desires would be frustrated, and power differences between the sexes would become the norm (Genesis 3:16). We see that damage, that brokenness of human relationships in many marriages today.

2. A second consequence was that the brokenness between them would lead to relational **distance**. Eve was told that she would have a desire for her husband

that could not be completely fulfilled, and that Adam would have a power that could be misused (Genesis 3:16). That dynamic replaced the mutuality that they originally shared in the Garden. Naturally, that created a tension between spouses that still affects us all today. We all know about couples that struggle with intimacy. We have seen marriages fall apart because of the slow drift away from each other. These disconnections are often rooted in our misdirected desires and power plays within marriage.

3. The final consequence was **death** (Genesis 3:19). Though Adam and Eve were created to share in an eternal relationship with their God, their choices brought an eventual end to relationships with God and each other through death. Couples still lose spouses through death today, but marriages also die through divorce. The marriage arena is often littered with the corpses of divorced and grieving spouses.

Consider what Adam and Eve's failure brought to marriage:

Damage: What was healthy and good became broken.

Distance: What was intended for intimacy and connection became fractured with unmet desires, misunderstanding, power, and conflict.

Death: What was intended to be life-giving has been ravaged by relational rupture (from discord to divorce).

These consequences have flowed down through the ages. Marriage has suffered and continues to suffer the results of the curse. Let's look at how these themes have rippled throughout marriage across centuries.

Marriage has served various purposes through the centuries; ancient cultures celebrated marriage as a natural act. Roman and Greek law formed around protecting marriage as an economic and childbearing unit. Sexual monogamy was not always common, as men often had sexual partners outside of marriage; wives primarily served a childbearing role. As diversity and wealth spread in the medieval and renaissance ages, marriage often carried value as monetary and social status benefits. It was important to marry into the right family, and to consider the potential wealth gained by the marriage. With the rise of the Catholic church, marriage became increasingly managed by the church. Decisions to marry or end a marriage were under the purview of the church alone. The Protestant Reformation gradually handed marriage over to management by governments.[3] That was the beginning of the western secularization of marriage.

More modern interpretations of marriage have emphasized sexual and personal fulfillment advantages. In today's American culture, marriage has undergone its most dramatic changes, all under the premise of social progress. But history has shown that all such interventions and changes have been misguided and inadequate. Marriage was never established for economic benefit, social power, or personal emotional fulfillment.

3 Witte, J., From *Sacrament to Contract - Marriage, Religion, and Law in the Western Tradition*, 2nd Ed. (Westminster John Knox Press; 2012).

No government, law, or social movement can sufficiently shape the sacred purposes of marriage. None of these interventions has adequately addressed the damage, distance, or death experienced by many in marriage. Regulations by churches and governments have proven unable to heal the damage to marriage. In fact, the Church—that should be marriage's greatest protector and promoter—has often failed to steward its purpose. Marriage continues to suffer the ailments of a broken world and creation.

The Current Problem

I see two primary problems in our current cultural view of marriage. First, we tend to see marriage as essential for healthy development and emotional stability. Our western culture has promoted marriage as the pinnacle of relational achievement. And many Christ-followers have compounded this problem by idolizing marriage. The message from media (and even pulpits) declares that true fulfillment and self-actualization are realized in finding your soulmate and living happily ever after. In his defense of same-sex marriage, Supreme Court Justice Anthony Kennedy called marriage society's "oldest institution" and that without marriage, same-sex couples are "condemned to loneliness." He concluded his comments, "… marriage is essential to our most profound hopes and aspirations."[4] He reflected the view that marriage is essential to personal happiness.

4 OBERGEFELL ET AL. v. HODGES, DIRECTOR, OHIO DEPARTMENT OF HEALTH, ET AL., US Supreme Court, June 26, 2015. https://www.supreme-court.gov/opinions/14pdf/14-556_3204.pdf.

The second problem is the warring between the genders, which diminishes both the female and male nature. For example, males in television shows and commercials are often portrayed as silly, incompetent, or weak. Entertainment media often presents women as the most aggressive characters. We also see female dependence on males as unhealthy. Male traits are amplified in female characters, while traditional female traits (nurturing, mothering, more emotionally expressive) are celebrated when they appear in male characters. The result is confusion and a diminishing of the distinct nature of males and females.

Churches have not helped. Not only have churches long promoted an entrenched patriarchy, but we've also heard too many pastors joke about gender stereotypes that feed the gender wars. The fights in churches over male/female leadership are horrible battlefields that have wounded and scarred. They have created division and caused many to even walk away from their faith. The competition between the genders (patriarchy, feminism, etc.) has only diminished the uniqueness, beauty, strength, wonder, and value of both men and women. We should celebrate these differing qualities in marriage.

In our efforts to find happiness and meet our "profound hopes and aspirations," many have been left feeling injured, traumatized, abandoned, and depressed. Men and women are increasingly in conflict. The battles about gender equality seem to have become more vitriolic. That has led society to redefine marriage—If marriage is failing, then maybe same-sex marriage, cohabitation, or multiple sexual partners would be reasonable solutions. My concern as a therapist is that we have placed the wrong expectations on marriage.

Let's consider same-sex marriage as a reflection of the titanic shift in cultural values. I believe this dramatic change has strong connections to the problems identified above. The first is our societal priority on individual self-fulfillment: "I will do what is best for me." Our culture emphasizes that true joy and contentment come from meeting your own needs first. Many self-help books, media, and some churches promote the message that you can find love in the type of relationship that makes you happy. So if your desires are for someone of the same sex, then fulfill those desires.

The second shift comes in the devaluing of the uniqueness of both genders in our culture. Patriarchy and feminism are still locked in a bitter war. Christians and church leaders have a responsibility to help model a healthier view. But in the meantime, same-sex marriage has been offered as a challenge to the patriarchy of traditional marriage; our culture proposes it as an equally viable way to find human connection. So most arguments, especially in church circles, for same-sex marriage center on:

1. Desire. "Same-sex attraction is a desire I was born with, so God would not want me to miss out." This idea is also intertwined to the secular and scientific promotion that sex is a need that should be fulfilled.
2. Loneliness. "God created us to be relational creatures, and same-sex marriage is the ideal way to solve my loneliness problem."

This culture's celebration and equating of same-sex marriage with heterosexual marriage is part of what is broken. If you would like a thoughtful and challenging exploration of these issues from a deeper scriptural study, I highly recommend *Two Views on Homosexuality, the Bible, and the Church* (Zondervan, 2016).

Self-fulfillment, "doing what makes me happy" and the lack of mutual respect for the unique genders has damaged marriage. To take marriages deeper, we must move from self-fulfillment to self-sacrifice and celebrate gender distinctions rather than fueling conflict.

Churches Need a Revolution

I believe many believers contribute to the diminishment of marriage. Marriage was never and should never be a secular institution, though we have allowed our society to shape marriage. Evidence shows that the early Protestant reformers handed much of the responsibility for marriage over to local governments rather than the church regulating marriage. The reformers intended to build a better society, allowing government to promote the values of the church.[5] God established marriage at creation, but large portions of the church have abdicated responsibility for promoting and holding couples to the high and sacred standards of marriage.

In 2014, the American Journal of Sociology published a study on the impact of conservative Protestantism on divorce rates.[6] The study claimed that divorce rates in counties with

---

5   Witte, J., From *Sacrament to Contract - Marriage, Religion, and Law in the Western Tradition*, 2nd Ed. (Westminster John Knox Press; 2012).

6   Jennifer Glass and Philip Levchak, *Red States, Blue States, and Divorce: Understanding the Impact of Conservative Protestantism on Regional Variation in*

high concentrations of conservative Protestants were higher because religious expression created higher divorce risks (marriage and childbearing at younger ages). The study argued that the proof is clear in the divorce rates of these counties. It is true that earlier marriages are at higher risk for divorce, but the reasons have more to do with emotional and financial stability (which increase with age). Pressing young Christian couples too quickly into marriage can be counterproductive.

The study revealed another large factor that contributes to the higher divorce rate—the level of religious involvement. Nominal Protestants had a much higher (almost double) divorce rates than more committed church-going couples. A married couple's level of religious commitment plays a crucial role in their long-term marriage stability.

The American Journal of Sociology study also validates that deeper religious practice is a necessity for stronger, more stable marriages. Church leaders need to set boundaries and reclaim the foundations of marriage as coming from God the Creator in the very beginning. We will not successfully promote the true values of marriage through the legislature. Though we can and should support legislation protecting marriage and the family, that cannot be our primary means for protecting what God created. The true call for what is right, good, and holy about marriage should come from pulpits and not from politicians. We have it backward. Rather than pushing a social agenda from Washington DC, we should allow our social agendas for marriage in our local church communities to be the yeast in the dough (Matthew 13:33).

Divorce Rates, American Journal of Sociology. Vol. 119, No. 4 (January 2014), pp. 1002-1046.

Knowing the history of marital impairment and breakage would help us understand the damage, distance, and death that have impacted marriage since the Garden. We need a shift in perspective for marriage that can bring us closer to God's intent for marriage from the beginning. We need to experience marriage as a *vocation*.

Marriage as Vocation

The word "vocation" means "calling," and has traditionally been interpreted as a call to Christian ministry. Current cultural use of the word focuses on work. Both interpretations only partially represent the views of the New Testament. The early followers of Jesus saw calling as being "all in." Their decision to make Jesus Lord was the "calling" on the whole of their life. (I Peter 2:9-10; I Corinthians 1:24; 26; Romans 8:30).

"By his divine power, God has given us everything we need for living a godly life. We have received all of this by coming to know him, the one who **called** (emphasis mine) us to himself by means of his marvelous glory and excellence… So dear brothers and sisters, work hard to prove that you really are among those God has called and chosen. Do these things, and you will never fall away." (2 Peter 1:3,10)

Most of us subdivide our lives. We have our marriage, family, work, church, recreation, and other compartments of life. We understand being called to be a Christian, but often that "calling" stops at the boundaries of the church parking lot. We may celebrate the call to mission work, but rarely consider that God might have called some to a "secular" vocation. In other words, many Christians see Peter's message as only applying to "church" life.

We rarely talk about marriage as a *calling*. I cannot remember any wedding ceremony (including my own) that mentions a "calling" to marriage or viewing marriage as a vocation. Our culture does not want to view marriage as work. We want marriage to be easy, we look for partners to be great matches, and we even live together before marriage to test-drive it. We try to reassure ourselves and society that the work will not be hard.

I am proposing the revolutionary idea that we view marriage as a vocation. We need to feel called into marriage as a part of our Christian walk. Our obedience to the calling of Christ pulls everything into submission to His Lordship. Paul argued that this was the case with marriage. In the earliest days of the church, many couples had divided faith households. One partner believed in Jesus, and the other partner remained a Jew, practiced pagan worship, or had no faith at all. Paul had direct advice for those divided marriages; stay in them. In other words, when you were "called" into faith with Jesus, marriage came as a part of the deal. In following Jesus, marriage became part of the vocation of faith.

"Don't you wives realize that your husbands might be saved because of you? And don't you husbands realize that your wives might be saved because of you? Each of you should continue to live in whatever situation the Lord has placed you, and remain as you were when God first **called** (emphasis mine) you. This is my rule for all the churches." (I Corinthians 7:16-17)

The American Journal of Sociology study identified two very important characteristics of the Christian community that seem to contribute to divorce rates: 1) Marriages that are not ready (the couple is too young) and 2) Marriages that lack a serious commitment to their faith (nominal Christians). Marriage as vocation improves both issues. When couples soberly examine and grasp marriage as a vocational calling, they can commit with greater maturity. Most will also demonstrate a higher level of faith commitment. Rather than seeing marriage as a legal contract, they are more likely to consider marriage as an act of their faith and a calling on their lives. Treating marriage as a vocation is far more than the legislated "covenant marriages" in Arizona, Arkansas, and Louisiana. Although those stricter marriage laws tend to be chosen by religious couples, they do little to elevate marriage as a vocation or calling.

Churches will also be less inclined to push marriage at younger ages. Many Christians no longer expect sexual purity from teenagers. We either don't talk about purity, just assuming it is happening, or we hurry young couples to marry so they will stop sinning. It is almost like you hear the collective sigh of relief at weddings: "Well, at least they are legal now."

But, we should express a strong and articulate sexual ethic in our churches, one that calls all members to holy living. That could provide a framework and space for conversations that could help individuals deepen their faith through marriage.

Christians, using revolutionary language, can reclaim the holy nature of marriage. We can pull it back from the unholy territory. When we explore God's higher ground for marriage, we discover marriage as a vocation, a serious calling to a serious spiritual act.

Conclusion

This sacred nature of marriage became corrupted and remains that way today. Look at the contrast of "no shame" (Genesis 2:25) and "felt shame" (Genesis 3:7). What a dramatic turn. The sacred became soiled. Safety and stability became corrupted by selfishness and competition. All the rest of scripture points to that brokenness and envisions the restoration of what failed in the Garden. That includes marriage. Sin in human relationships constricts God's creation. Therefore, Paul says creation "groans" to be released to the freedom it once enjoyed. Sin constricts marriage when men and women diminish and devalue their gifts. Sin also inhibits marriage when men and women choose selfishness over submission.

Revolutionary marriage elevates the sacred nature of marriage. Marriage as a vocation sees the redemption of what sin defaced to what God intended. The human history of marriage has shown glimpses of what God designed in Eden. We witness the vignettes of sacredness when the diversity and uniqueness of maleness and femaleness are celebrated. In a revolutionary marriage, couples embrace oneness through sacrifice and submission. We can all point to honorable and beautiful examples of Christian marriage. I wrote this book to provide support to your marriage, helping it model the holy covenant needed in our communities. Chapter 3 is a richer exploration of how marriage can move from the realm of the unholy to the sacred.

REFOCUS

Marriage as a vocation or calling represents the central idea in this chapter. That means marriage holds the potential to draw couples into deeper faith and holiness. That also means helping others build faith as they witness God's grace at work in marriage. Consider how your marriage can serve both functions—personal faith development and witness to the world.

Purpose

I wrote this book to help you lay a foundation for the vocational call of your marriage. To do that well, I believe it helps to explore the core values which undergird your marriage. Don't assume everyone understands them. They don't. Bring them into the light of examination.

Plan

Make sure you sanctify the time for this activity. Schedule the time and place to be free of time constraints and distractions. Make sure you approach the time prayerfully and in the right mindset. These activities are not intended to provide a solution for a specific conflict. If you face a disagreement, try to set that issue aside. If you cannot do that, work out a resolution first, and then come back to this conversation. This activity will probably take 60 minutes or more. This is important; make sure you prepare and protect the time necessary to dig deep.

SO WHAT'S NEXT?

Practice

1. I recommend that each of you make a list of 3-5 core values you see as essential to your marriage; the character, attitudes, and behaviors you want to fill up in your home, church, work, and community. These values can be one word (I.e. commitment, love, sacrifice, etc.) or a phrase (I.e. sexually faithful, share quality time and adventures, empathic listening, etc.)

2. Write a sentence or two to describe each value and why it is important.

3. Share your lists with each other. Be sure to share your whole list before listening to your partner's list. Listen for the whole picture of what each of you is trying to present in your list of values. Notice the areas of agreement.

4. Create a marriage values statement. Choose the values (from your lists) that you both agree are essential for your marriage. Write down each value and describe in a sentence or two how that value will be displayed in your marriage. For example, "Submission—We will consider the needs of 'the other' as higher priority than our personal needs."

5. Write down and display this values statement in your home. Place it in a location where it can be found, reviewed, revisited, and revised as necessary.

Chapter 3
Sacred Marriage

"Why did I marry her?" Sam's voice was hollow over the phone. The marriage was only three years old, and Sam was wondering if there was any chance to salvage it. He told me they fought all the time. He didn't know if she would be open to marriage counseling.

But, Tammi agreed to meet, even though her heart had been broken, and she wasn't sure she wanted to remain in the marriage. She felt betrayed. In counseling, she said she never knew Sam had so many quirks that would need to be satisfied for him to be content. He wanted things his way. For example, he insisted his clothes be hung a certain way, and he would not allow certain foods in the home. He could have spectacular tantrums when his conditions were not met. Tammi's frustrations confused Sam. Tammi now criticized some things about Sam that she loved when they were dating. Although she admired his financial skills when she first met him, in marriage she felt he was stingy with money. Before marriage she valued his calm confidence in a crisis. But, now she saw that as weak and passive.

What happened in the Garden?

God created marriage. The relationship between Adam and Eve in the Garden gives a framework for understanding God's intentions for marriage. Consider the two tellings of human creation in scripture. The first (Genesis 1:26-31) looks at God making man in His own image, male and female. In the second telling (Genesis 2:7-25), God created Adam first. After naming all the animals, Adam (and God!) knew none of them would be a suitable mate. So God caused him to fall asleep, removed a rib, and from it created Eve. When Adam awoke and saw Eve, he declared his contentment with her. And, God said that was why a man would leave his father and mother, choose his wife, and the two would become one. Those two versions deliver specific messages about men, women, and marriage. Jesus even used both narratives to teach on marriage (Mark 10: 6-9). Because Jesus talked about marriage in the Garden, let's look at the messages found in the Garden narrative about marriage.

The first is that God designed males and females to equally reflect His nature (Genesis 1:26-27; 2:18). One literal translation of Genesis 2:18 reads, "It is not good for man to be alone. I will make him a helper **who is his equal** (emphasis mine)."[7] Second, the narrative tells us an essential component of marriage is the denial of self and ultimately the death of self (Genesis 2:23-25). The "oneness" referenced in verse 24 is much more than a sexual reference. Becoming "one" means the self-identity must die to make a new identity in marriage. Marriage is a path of sacrifice; we give up our own needs and desires for the good of the other. These are the revolutionary ideas foundational in this book. Marriage, as God designed it, honors the image-bearing people in the relationship. It also brings death to individuality, so that the community will witness the power of submission, sacrifice, and grace. These acts of worship, the vocation of marriage, bring glory to God; His image-bearing creatures honored by spouses and God's grace are lived out in the daily sacrifices of husband and wife.

Geometry of Marriage

The debate in Christian circles about marriage roles often centers around male-female differences and gender roles. Those who write about this topic typically fall into one of two camps. The complementarians hold a more traditional view, suggesting that men and women have roles that "complement" each other, but are different as outlined in the Bible. This group often places men in roles of "spiritual authority." A second group, the egalitarians, see men and women equally serving in leadership roles (home or church) based on their

---

7 Dennis Prager, *The Rational Bible: Genesis* (Washington, D.C.; Regnery Faith, 2019).

spiritual gifting rather than gender. This group places an emphasis on gender equality.

The argument between these two sides has contributed to some of our problems with Christian marriage. Both perspectives make valid points, but both also ignore important biblical ideals. We can embrace the valid perspectives from both camps and discard the others.

The complementarians are correct to highlight gender difference and the unique gifting of males and females. But, their view falls short by creating an environment that often treats women as "less than." It also supports the misguided values of patriarchy. The egalitarians find solid footing to see males and females as equal "image-bearers" of the Creator. But sometimes they can overlook the distinctive qualities of both males and females. They often lose the exquisite artistry behind God's creation of what it means to be male and female.

This book promotes a new and revolutionary supplementarian idea, joining the good ideas of the complementarian and egalitarian views. Blending the two perspectives may take us closer to what God established in the beginning. Both groups belong at the same table.

In geometry, two angles that equal 90 degrees are complementary, one-quarter of a circle. Supplementary angles equal 180 degrees, half a circle. If we consider a circle as a model for completeness, then the supplementary angle view of marriage might be a better fit. Consider a particular spiritual gift, like joy, goodness, or patience, and let's map it for a hypothetical marriage. Spouses, male or female, are highly unlikely to have equal gifting of any one quality. A wife may be a better leader than her husband. A husband might be a better encourager/nurturer than his wife. But taken together, they add up to half of a circle. So, what about the other half? That is where God comes in. He completes what is incomplete. As the husband and wife live out their unique gifting, they reflect the nature of God in a mirror image.

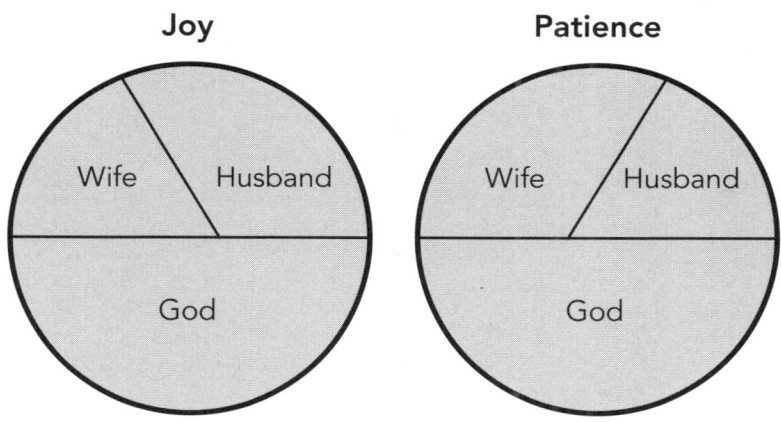

Males and Females - Congruent—Not Equal

As a marriage counselor, I sadly and often hear accusations of spouses. The accuser wants to show his or her spouse as "less than." These words, spoken from pride, superiority, and contempt, show the speaker has lost respect for his or her partner. Those accusations also depersonalize their spouse; they devalue what they once believed him or her to be. But, a sacred marriage should regain and maintain the value and dignity of each partner.

After declaring Adam and Eve were higher in nature than any other living creature, God announced for the first time that everything was "very good (Gen. 1:26-31)." That story tells us that men and women are both created in the image of God. That validates gender differences and that each gender is equal as an image-bearer of God. Furthermore, God described what He made as "very good." Maleness and femaleness are very good things, or as the New Living Translation states, "excellent in every way." Neither is better than, more competent than, or greater than the other. The supplementary nature of men and women reflects the image of God.

Eve was not an afterthought. And, Adam was not a failed first try, with Eve being the new improved model. Let's consider the scientific and scriptural evidence of this supplementary nature of the genders.

1. Neurological evidence suggests unique skills and abilities between the genders (see the list below).
2. The biological anatomy of our genitalia reflects a design intended to fit in a symbiotic connection.
3. The second creation narrative emphasized the "created for" nature of the male-female relationship.
4. When asked about divorce in marriage, Jesus affirmed the supplementary nature of males and females. He did not directly address or endorse the patriarchy of marriage that was so prevalent during that time (Matthew 19:4-6).
5. In Ephesians 5, Paul highlighted mutual submission as a founding principle for marriage, illustrated by Christ's death and the church's submission to Christ. In Ephesians 5:21, He told spouses to mutually submit.

Scientific research has identified many brain differences between males and females. Some differences that contribute to supplementary gifts and abilities are below:

1. The corpus callosum (brain tissue connecting two halves of the brain) is much thicker and denser in females. As a result, men tend to be left-brain dominant, and women shift between thoughts and information quicker.
2. The increased tissues between the two halves give women a slightly greater language ability, but men are better able to focus.
3. The fight-or-flight response in men is stronger, possibly connected to a larger amygdala. That supports their strong protective nature.
4. The richer neural networks in the limbic system of a female brain allow greater emotional expression and social connection.
5. Women have larger concentrations of oxytocin receptors in the brain, leading to increased social bonding and nurturing responses.
6. Men generally have improved spatial skills.
7. Men may be more prone to dyslexia, language challenges, ADHD, and autism - Women are more prone to mood disorders such as anxiety and depression.

These differences are most evident when examining large populations. In fact, some research shows that when we look at small groups or individuals, there are blends of neurological strengths and weaknesses. Some men can have feminine qualities and some women can have masculine characteristics. But even with these variations, the different "giftings" of the genders are consistent across a population. God created men and women to be different. That truth has been consistent for all time. I have seen marriages where the differences don't show along traditional male and female lines. In fact, in our marriage, Patricia and I know (and joke about) my more female qualities (talkative, social, emotional). A sacred marriage honors the unique and supplementary gifts of each spouse regardless of how they fall along male and female boundaries.

In marriage, each spouse should create a sacred space where these differences are honored and valued. We refuse to use marital stereotypes (wives' struggles with driving directions or husbands' failure to focus) as battering rams to demean or shame each other. A wife's ability to understand and nurture her children compensates for her lack of spatial skills. A husband's focus challenge is balanced by his ability to remain calm in a crisis. God created men and women to help each other. By valuing and honoring our differences (strengths and weaknesses), we become better.

Geometrically, we might describe this as congruent rather than equal. In mathematical terms, "equality" means precisely "the same." That is untrue for males and females. In mathematics, congruent is an equality that allows angles and shapes to be the same in size and degrees. But, they may have a different orientation or be on a different plane. This is a better description for married spouses. Males and females are uniform image-bearers but accomplish this goal with different means.

Each couple's unique fingerprint of differences is beautiful. I am always amazed to see the infinite combination of skills, gifts, and temperaments in each marriage I counsel. I never feel the need to tell men to be more manly or women to be more feminine. The way each couple "fits" together is beautiful just as God designed them. In a sacred marriage, a husband celebrates and honors his wife's gifts. He does not bemoan or complain about how she could be different. In a sacred marriage, a wife respects and delights in her husband's unique skills. She does not criticize or demean when he comes up short.

But, wait. Didn't Eve come from Adam's rib? Didn't Peter call females the weaker sex? Didn't Paul imply that wives need to submit to male authority because the wife is at fault for sin?

The short answer to these questions is "yes," and many books have taken deep dives into each of those scriptures. Sometimes, we have to separate cultural issues from spiritual ones. The egalitarian nature of marriage in our western culture was nonexistent in New Testament times and cultures. Women were second-class citizens; they were not even allowed the same level of education as men. Consider the cultural significance of the New Testament reflecting a patriarchal view. Peter and Paul may have been suggesting that believers be careful about their witness to the community at large. As you will see in the following examples, they encouraged equality. But they did not want couples or churches to promote such radical behavior that the message of Jesus was lost in controversy.

For example, in I Peter 3:1-7, Peter told wives to accept the authority of their husbands. That sounds harsh to our modern western ears. But, let's step into the shoes of the first-century Christians. Peter described how believers model submission to authority. He had already talked about submitting to government and slaves submitting to masters before he turned to the family. Remember that in that time and place, men were the educated ones, and many women were followers of Christ, but their husbands were not. What was a woman to do? Was she supposed to point out her husband's errors when she wasn't educated and was already treated as a second-class citizen? Peter's message encouraged an environment in the home that submitted to the current cultural power structures, possibly winning over the husbands to their wife's faith in Christ. Their humble submission reflects the ancient humility of Sarah, who followed Abraham.

We must consider the context when we read any scripture. In a culture that demeaned women, Peter told believing husbands to treat their wives with honor. Peter called women "weaker," but remember they had less power and were less educated. Peter just acknowledged the cultural conditions in explaining why that made it necessary for husbands to treat wives in an understanding way. That was revolutionary for the time. Imagine a husband extending dignity to a wife whom the culture considered no better than a slave. The scriptures are full of countercultural ideas. The church of that time *was* a counterculture! And it should be today. And it would be if we lived out:

1. **What Jesus said about marriage**

   When asked about divorce in Mark 10:5-12, Jesus referenced Genesis 2:24 and then said that a man and woman commit adultery if they divorce their spouse to marry someone else. Although the culture at the time blamed women and excused the behavior of men, Jesus placed responsibility equally on men and women.

2. **Paul's statement about mutual submission**
   In Ephesians 5:21, Paul told men and women to equally submit to one another. He then explained how submission differs for each gender.

3. **Paul's statements about married sex** (I Cor. 7)
   Paul wrote that husbands and wives should not sexually deprive each other and that each should give the authority of their body to their spouse. Such an assumption of mutual submission was counter to their culture.

4. **Peter calls wives equal partners**
   In I Peter 3, Peter called wives to submit for the purpose of influencing their unbelieving husbands. He then called husbands to live with their wives in an understanding way. Most translations use the word "heirs" or "joint-heirs" to describe the marital union. An heir is an equal recipient of the inheritance. Peter even wrote that to do anything other than treat their wives as equals would hinder a husband's prayers.

5. **Women were significant participants and supports of the ministry of Jesus.**
   Jesus' teachings and practice valued women in ways that were revolutionary for the time.

I believe these scriptures support the revolutionary and supplementarian view of marriage presented in this book. I also believe that view is also well-suited to our western culture. If Christians lived that out daily, the sacred nature of marriage would be on full display. There is no place for gender wars in Christian marriage.

"Oneness" - Death of Self, not Self-Fulfillment

I also hear many versions of the blame game in my counseling:

"She is never interested in sex."

"He is always working and never listens when I ask him to come home."

"She spends way too much money."

"He spends too much time...."

John and Julie Gottman, prolific researchers in marriage, see those criticisms as the beginning seeds of contempt. Contempt is a marriage killer. It destroys a marriage because the focus is outward and blaming. It is fed by feelings of disgust and hostility. Those husbands and wives seem to have concluded they could find happiness if only their partner would change. They have become blind to their own contributions to problems in the marriage. They seek self-satisfaction.

God never designed or intended marriage to be a platform for satisfying self. In fact, He designed it for the exact opposite reason. In the Genesis 2 telling of God's creation of males and females, God created Eve by taking a part from Adam's side. Sacrifice was required to find the joy of companionship. The "oneness" referenced in Gen. 2:24 was not just sexual. It referred to unity and wholeness. This Hebrew word has been translated in other places as "same," "common," "together," and "alike." Two parts are no longer alone, but they have made something new. The marriage and union of two people is something more, something greater than either of them could be alone. But, it requires the death of the self.

In Ephesians 5, Paul used the relationship between Christ and the church to illustrate the mysterious unity of marriage. He challenged wives to submit to their husbands "in everything." He commanded husbands to love their wives like Christ loved the church, "giving up His life for her." In both cases, the language projects totality. It demands complete commitment and full sacrifice. Submission in marriage means giving up self.

The Gottmans offer solutions for the harmful effects of criticism and contempt in marriage. They talk about bids for connection that receive a response of "turning away" or "turning towards." Contempt and criticism turn away from connection. Turning towards a partner requires sacrifice. It is a stance of openness, listening, and engagement. It also means that when dealing with problems in marriage, spouses refuse to assign blame. Each owns his or her parts of the difficulties and accepts the direction of the spouse. It also means choosing vulnerability and sharing needs and feelings rather than pointing out the other's faults. Paul said the same thing in Ephesians 5:33 - "So again I say, each man must love his wife as he loves himself, and the wife must respect her husband."

What Makes Marriage Sacred?

Marriage, at its best, is a symbolic representation of God's perfect love for His people. When imperfect husbands and wives join in the unity of marriage, they arrive at an opportunity to model His perfect love. The Gottman research has revealed that 69% of problems in marriage are perpetual[8]; there are no solutions. Two broken people face the need to figure out how to live with the ongoing difficulty. The only way that can happen is for grace to fill the space between them. A spouse treating his or her partner as a unique and equal image-bearer of the Creator reveals God's love. The same thing happens when a spouse lays down personal interests, desires, wishes, and needs, to prefer and honor the partner's interests. These two postures disclose the sacred vocation of marriage. Together, as one, male and female, dying to self, elevating their partners to be purer image-bearers of their Creator. That is what God intended in Eden.

I want to be very clear here. The core concept of this book is that marriage is a chosen path for living out your faith. Marriage is not about self-fulfillment; it is not some pinnacle of self-actualization. It is the exact opposite, a chosen vocation of self-sacrifice. That's why this book stands in direct contrast to the cultural messages and promotion of self-fulfillment so evident in our culture.

Tammi and Sam worked hard to change the poor habits in their marriage. Tammi began to appreciate and compliment the gifts Sam brought to the marriage. Sam began to see how his desires blinded him to Tammi's needs. The language of sacrifice and unity entered their marriage.

We will take these two ideas (male/female complementarity and "oneness") and weave them throughout the rest of this book. We will look at safe, stable, and successful marriage:

8   John M. Gottman, *The Science of Trust — Emotional Attunement for Couples* (New York, W.W. Norton and Company, 2011).

- Chapter 4 will look at the biblical concept of forgiveness, being known, and the value of vulnerability in a Safe Marriage.
- Chapter 5 will go deeper into commitment to see how it provides for a Stable Marriage.
- Chapter 6 will consider what really makes a Successful Marriage. We will look into the sacred space of grace between a husband and wife.

Are you ready to join the revolution?

RENEW

To call marriage "sacred" is to acknowledge its holy nature, and to allow the practice of being married to make us holy. This chapter has been about the deeper spiritual components of marriage, drawing us into intimacy with our spouse and intimacy with God. Part of the holiness of marriage is that it starts with a covenant.

Purpose

Marriage vows form a significant part of the foundation built between husband and wife. You may have spoken traditional vows (used since medieval times) in your wedding, similar to these:

I, ___, take thee, ___, to be my wedded husband/wife, to have and to hold, from this day forward, for better, for worse, for richer, for poorer, in sickness and in health, to love and to cherish, till death do us part, according to God's holy ordinance; and thereto I pledge thee my faith [or] pledge myself to you.

Other couples have composed their own vows or some variation of the above. Whatever was used, they all contain agreements and commitments.

I designed this exercise to revisit your vows. Sometimes the foundation needs to be inspected to ensure that it remains solid. We often need to restate and reaffirm those promises, giving us a chance to renew our commitments.

SO WHAT'S NEXT?

Plan

Set aside plenty of time for this activity. Do your best to eliminate distractions. You will need to work in advance to get ready for the activity. Give yourself plenty of time for that.

Pre-work: Read and reflect on the vows—traditional or personalized—shared in your wedding. Try to locate the specific vows used. Ask yourself the following questions:

1. What remains true about these vows? How have they been lived out?
2. What would you change about the vows? Having been married for some time, would you change them or add anything to clarify the promises needed in your marriage?
3. Rewrite your vows. It might be useful to refer back to the core values exercise from the last chapter to help identify a starting point. What promises do you want to renew with each other? What new promises do you want to make? There is no right or wrong for the length of the vows. What is important is that they still communicate what is important. This activity will probably need some focused time over several days. Individually you might need several sessions to sit and reflect. This is important, so make sure you have set aside the time to dig deep.

Practice

Schedule a time to share these new vows with each other. Share them privately or before witnesses. Ceremony can be important, so it may be more meaningful to speak them before close friends.

Make sure it is in a setting will permit you to look at each other face to face. Speak them out loud. Make sure you look into each other's eyes as you share the agreements and commitments. Save what you vowed to each other so you can revisit other times in the future.

This is an opportunity for renewal. It should give you a chance as a couple to remind each other of what has been important and what you hope to make important going forward.

Chapter 4

Safe Marriage – From Damage to Reconciliation

*R*obert's sales rep position required frequent travel over a large multi-state territory. And, a woman he supervised joined him on some of the trips. Their affair started, like too many, under the influence of alcohol. Although he awakened from his moral failure, haunting consequences appeared and then intensified—threatening emails, anonymous texts, and threats of legal action and job loss. Robert's wife, Gina, was terrified when she called me.

Gina and Robert both described their marriage as "distant." Robert tried to justify his behavior by the lack of sexual contact with Gina. At the deepest point of the affair, he decided to leave his marriage and live with his coworker. That's when the secret messages to Gina started. At first, she did not believe them. Though she knew their marriage was not perfect, she never thought Robert would cheat on her. But then the photos of Robert kissing this other woman blew the lid off. When Gina confronted him with the proof, he admitted everything.

Robert didn't want to lose his family, so he agreed to end the affair. But that decision did not end the pervasive threats and worry. Soon, they learned their family was being stalked. Fear and concerns for their safety became a primary focus of therapy.

I worked with Robert and Gina to evaluate the threats, establish boundaries, and increase their sense of security. Rebuilding marital and familial safety took lots of work. But, a sense of safety was essential.

Safety is a crucial but endangered reality in our culture. The evening newscasts carry ominous reports of dark threats and violence lurking within our communities. The increasing perception of risks from school shootings, riots, terrorism, or viral outbreaks increase our anxiety and stress levels. We feel an almost continuous need to be "on guard." Our brains respond to these modern life hazards by seeking safety. And though protecting our families is important, hyper-vigilance is not always helpful. Obviously, we cannot ignore the danger. But overreacting to threats is riskier. When we insulate ourselves from danger, the results often disconnect and isolate us from our relationships.

Seeking safety is a reaction rooted in the pesky amygdala. That is the little gland buried deep in the center of our brains; it activates our flight-fight-or-freeze response when we feel threatened. It is essential for survival. It has its place, but overuse can be a problem. It can lead to withdrawal and increased conflict in relationships, rather than protecting us. The real or imagined conflicts of modern life can overwork our amygdala and make us afraid when there is nothing to fear. Trying to live in a cocoon of safety, avoiding all risks, can bring disconnection to our marriage and family relationships. The slow creep of stress can lead to emotional distance and even the loss of the marriage.

Marriage is messy. Two imperfect human beings sharing space will develop heightened emotional stress responses. It is impossible to escape that reality. But, when couples try to build a "safe" marriage that avoids stress and conflict at all cost, they can end up with a weak, shaky relationship that can easily fall apart. Sadly, they build a marriage that cannot be tested by life. On the other end of a continuum, some couples expose their marriage to unnecessary risks—substance abuse, financial mismanagement, or sexual infidelity–to escape the conflicts of the home. The results from either end of the continuum bring new and more intense conflicts and instability, often resulting in the death of the marriage.

So how do we find a balance with stress and risk?

We must learn to live in the mess of marriage without disconnection and threat. A safe marriage requires secure and stable supports. And, we need to know how to take risks. To develop this revolutionary strategy, we need to explore the idea of attachment. What are those deep bonds we share as humans? How do they shape us?

Attachments - The Good, The Bad, The Messy

To understand safety within the husband and wife bonds, we need to go back to the bond between infant and parent. Attachment theory—developed in the 1950s and well-established as a way to understand human connections—sees that bonds in family relationships are shaped by instinctual neurological drives. Those drives function much like our drive for food or sleep. They encourage us to seek comfort and safety when we feel stressed or insecure. From the moment our girls were born, they would turn to the sound of their mother's voice. The attachment dance between a parent and child starts in these initial moments and continues through the years.

A child on the playground gives us a good picture of that attachment dance. Imagine a kindergartener at the playground; her mother sitting on a bench nearby. You see the child move away from Mom to explore the equipment, then she moves back to Mom to check-in, receive attention, and perhaps comfort for an injury. That dance of distance and closeness, the back and forth, helps the child develop confidence and a sense of stability because her source of safety, her engaged, attentive mom, sits on the bench nearby. She can return as necessary.

But, what if the parent is unavailable, distracted, unpleasant, or even rejecting? Sometimes, when connection does not happen, the child stops asking for it. There is no ebb and flow; Mom sits quietly or distracted on the bench, and the child plays alone on the playground.

To make that playground dance work requires risk and vulnerability. The child risks moving away from Mom even while trusting Mom's availability. And the child learns vulnerability by seeking reassurance and help as needed. The mom takes risks by allowing the child to venture out. But, Mom is also vulnerable in recognizing that she misunderstands sometimes, but she keeps trying to tune into the needs of her child. Occasional mismatches in her responses are normal; they can actually be helpful to fine-tuning the parent-child connection. I call them the "messy middle."

The benefit of the messy middle is that it creates greater opportunities to increase connection. That happens through the dance of vulnerability, forgiveness, and reconciliation. The child seeking help and the parent's response are both positions of vulnerability. If they are attuned to each other (child communicates a need, the parent understands), then all goes well. But, a mismatch and some dissonance (child doesn't know how to ask, parent is too busy to respond) leads to disconnection. In this mess, forgiveness keeps the door to vulnerability open. The parent has to be forgiving of the child's immaturity, and the child has to be forgiving of the parent's tuning her out. Because of forgiveness, the parent and child keep trying, and through vulnerable risks they fine-tune their connection and reconcile. Each little tuning step pulls the parent-child a bit closer into a symphony of deep connection.

Those experiences form a mental model about intimate relationships that we eventually carry into marriage. We see that dance in all close human relationships. As a marriage therapist, I apply that dynamic to husbands and wives.

What About the Piggy Banks?

We all carry attachment piggy banks in our heart. We have one for every intimate relationship in our life—our parents, siblings, best friends, and our spouses. We interpret the good things that happen, bringing safety and security to us, as deposits in that piggy bank. But, when an intimate relationship places excessive expectation, injures, or disappoints us, we see that as a withdrawal from the bank.

We carry distinct piggy banks for each person. The one for your father differs from the one for your mother. So, if your mother makes significant deposits, that has no effect on the balance in your father's piggy bank. And here is the kicker for kids—if the parental piggy banks are empty, there is nothing your spouse (or anyone else) can do to fill that empty bank. They cannot make it better. Yet, we often try to do that. We engage in close connections with others, including our spouses, in hopes of making deposits in certain piggy banks. It just won't work. It also won't work if your parental piggy banks are full, but your marriage runs a deficit of affection and emotional connection. The marital piggy bank will feel empty.

So, the marriage piggy bank gauges the depth of marital connection. Maintaining a positive surplus in the piggy bank reflects healthy bonds. Withdrawals and insufficient deposits build stress. Sometimes, changes in emotional balance of the piggy bank can be sudden, unexpected, and unintentional. Sometimes they are temporary and need to be endured until circumstances change. Many of these changes are normal, such as illness, children, changing jobs, or moves to new communities. But, stresses can often contribute to a cycle of withdrawal, requests for repayment, and finally disconnection. This cycle typically leads to emptier piggy banks, increased distrust and eventually emotional distance.

Keeping a positive balance between deposits and withdrawals requires an intentional effort to dance in the messy middle of attachment. Because our marital attachments are rarely in perfect tune, we adjust. That requires the vulnerability, forgiveness, and reconciliation dance in order to sustain the attachment bond.

Remember your spouse cannot make up for deficits in your relationship with your parents or other intimate relationships. If you have been injured in those relationships, you can only forgive the debt. You cannot expect other relationships to cover it. Forgiveness does not mean you will forget the injuries (the empty piggy bank never goes away), but it does mean you choose to give up the emotional pull to the debt. Forgiveness means you no longer demand deposits in the piggy bank, and you learn to cope with the empty bank. Please remember the forgiveness process may require work with a therapist.

So, let's say your parents fell at the good end of the responsive attachment spectrum. When you had a need, most of the time their response matched your need. If you marry someone who struggles with hearing or responding to needs, you may find the spouse relationship confusing and even painful. The opposite is also true. Let's say your parents were rarely available to respond to your needs. If your spouse hears your need and responds appropriately, you might not trust the response to be genuine or stable. That is part of the complexity of the messy middle.

Fear drives the breakdown of attachment in both cases. Fear of being alone, shamed, rejected, or injured. Fear can be cancerous, eventually bringing human disconnection. Jesus knew that. I think that's why he so often said, Do not be afraid." But Jesus did not call his followers to a risk-free life. He sent his disciples into places and situations that might bring them fear or rejection, but Jesus remained a source of security that the disciples could always return to for support. Jesus also took risks by trusting His mission to His followers.

The marriage relationship is a mirror of the connection that Jesus has with His followers. This level of risk is necessary for deep connection. Because when we stop taking risks, we withdraw from being vulnerable. Safe marriage requires risk and vulnerability from both parties.

Safe Marriage Requires Vulnerability

To be understood is one of our greatest human needs. We just want to feel like someone "gets us." When someone (parent, friend, spouse) understands us, we feel comforted, and a sense of peace. When we are misunderstood, we feel alone, distant, unknown and unsettled. Feeling known or understood motivates us to go deeper into the relationship, but misunderstanding and the lack of empathy make us disconnect. Relational moments that lack connection will increase feelings of shame, making us feel something is wrong with us. The path to increasing connections in marriage leads to increased vulnerability. That means clearly stating our needs and receiving the needs of our spouse. Vulnerability is a scary and risky position in marriage.

From various biblical passages, we see that sex is more than the joining of two bodies. It is part of a deeper intimacy. Biblical *knowledge* speaks of deeper connection and intimacy. When husbands and wives "know" each other, children are the result of the totality of intimacy in a marriage, not just the sexual act.

This Hebrew word for knowledge, "דַּעַת," was first used in Genesis 2:9, 17, referencing the tree of the knowledge of good and evil. God's restriction against the tree did not refer to information, but to intimacy. God was warning Adam and Eve against seeking their intimacy and provisions in the wrong places; Do not go 'know' something else. 'Know me.'" The result of their choice to "know" something apart from God resulted in deep shame—they hid.

That is precisely the danger in marriage when we choose to not be vulnerable with our partner, or we reject or neglect our partner's needs. That lack of intimacy brings shame and distance. The higher call in marriage is to know each other through acts of vulnerability and submission. That creates safety in marriage. It is foundational to the purposes of marriage.

The safety creates:

1. **Awareness of personal needs and the risk to express them**

   That invites us to present our true needs. Rather than pointing out the faults of our spouse, we can share what we need from him or her. Sharing needs requires submission and vulnerability; pointing out faults and disappointments is an act of control. To share my need means I open my heart with the risk of rejection or injury.

2. **Openness to hear and respond to spouse's needs above your own.**

   You should be open to hearing the needs of your spouse. To be open to his or her needs means I deny or crucify my own needs. That is an act of submission and taking the risk of making the wrong response in meeting those needs.

"Wait," you might say, "Who goes first? Who gets to state their needs and who denies their desires?" That line of questioning suggests that marriage is tit-for-tat, you scratch my back, then I'll scratch yours. But, the expression and the response are simultaneous acts by both partners. Remember, marriage is sacred because of the death of self-fulfillment. If you simultaneously present your needs with a heart towards hearing and meeting the needs of your spouse, you create a space of safety. That is a true position of vulnerability and submission.

Safe Marriage Requires Forgiveness

That can all go wrong if we hold back on sharing our needs and do not meet our spouse's requests for help. When I choose not to reveal, I withdraw. When I chose not to receive, I defend or dismiss. Both failures, disconnection and defensiveness, require a spirit of grace and forgiveness. First, we all struggle with vulnerability. Remember the messiness of attachment? We have all been injured in the past. That can make us cautious about stating our needs; we don't want to be dismissed or rejected. Second, our spouses will sometimes fail to meet our needs. Remember the parent who missed the cues and needs of her child on the playground?

So, the gap between vulnerability, intimacy, disconnection, and defensiveness is where the real work of marriage occurs. In that gap is where we accept and own our personal shortcomings and those of our spouse. That sacred space is where we admit our faults and work on self-forgiveness. It is also where we share the hurts from our spouse, and work on forgiveness of him or her. Forgiveness means the piggy bank carries an overdraft. But, after sharing and owning that debt, we then choose to forgive the debt.

That means once we have talked through the injury, disconnection or loss, we decide to stop reminding ourselves and our spouse of the debt. We choose to treat them as if the obligation never happened. That place is risky because we return to a state of vulnerability; we might get injured again. Jesus told His followers that they should forgive 70 times 7, meaning an infinite amount. If He said that we should do that for our brother (or neighbor), how much more should we do it for our spouse?

Safe Marriage requires Submission and Vulnerability–Reconciliation

So, what does all this look like in a marriage? How do we find safety in marriage? What do intimacy and vulnerability look like?

Just as a diamond reveals its deep beauty and brilliance when viewed against black velvet, sometimes we can best behold the radiance of marriage against the dark backdrop of infidelity.

As we all know, an affair, emotional or sexual, is one of the most significant offenses in marriage. That's because it is so clearly connected to our values around marriage as our most intimate relationship. It is that state where we are "known" the best. I have counseled many couples ensnared in that trap. Sadly, affairs are increasing and leading to increasing divorce statistics. Many factors contribute to the increase of affairs, including our culture's' hedonistic worship of sex, an increase in impersonal social connections through electronics and social media, the easy and secret availability of pornography, and increased social acceptance of affairs as a norm.

In my experience, I have seen that we sow the seeds to a blossoming affair through disconnection and defensiveness. They grow from the lack of vulnerability and forgiveness. In my therapy work, I have yet to find a couple who could not identify the beginnings of an affair as tied to some emotional disconnections and relational defensiveness in the marriage.

The work of forgiveness in marital affairs is enormous and takes time, but it is essential to creating a safe space for

1) vulnerability to return, and 2) reconciliation to begin. And, forgiveness starts with naming the injury. It is important for the couple to talk through the offense. The level of detail discussed will vary by situation, but the injured person benefits when he or she gives voice to the pain. The next step requires an acknowledgment of the injury. The offender's submission, humility, and lack of defensiveness communicates that he or she owns the injuries created. They acknowledge what they did. The transgressor offers no defense or excuse, and that becomes the moment that forgiveness can begin. Begin. Forgiveness is a process, whether a couple is working on forgiveness of an affair, or a wife needs to forgive a husband for leaving the toilet seat up. The process emerges from the decision to not have the offender pay for the offense anymore.

Our culture assumes that an affair is the last nail in the coffin for a marriage. And though it may have to be the case (especially when the offender refuses to repent), it does not have to be. Revolutionary marriages model forgiveness first. Yes, that's a hard path, but necessary to build a safe marriage. Both partners risk vulnerability again. The spouse who had the affair chooses to be vulnerable by confessing their failure and submitting to higher accountability. The spouse victimized by the affair forgives and works toward rebuilding trust. The obvious risk here is being vulnerable to future rejection.

When I have sat with couples at that tender, risky spot, I have often seen it to be a sacred space. A husband bowed in shame, owning his selfish choices over a one-night stand. A wife feels humiliated, tearfully sharing how she got caught up in the emotional whirlwind of an online affair with a high school boyfriend. The offended spouse, whether husband or wife, refuses to judge or attack. They listen, empathize, and decide to forgive. At that moment everything slows down, and I feel like I am standing on a precipice, staring into eternity.

I can see I am witnessing a mystery, a place where the values of the world turn upside down. Where there should be injury, I see healing. Where there should be disconnection, I see communion. Where there should be anger, I see acceptance.

That is reconciliation. It means the deficits in the piggy banks are paid, the books rebalanced, and both parties start at the same place. Couples suffering through affair recovery know it's a hard journey. It takes time and commitment to remain vulnerable, continuing to forgive, and reconciling in sacred spaces. But, we cannot wait until we have big offenses like an affair to experience the sacred, intimate connections. Reconciliation needs to happen in the smallest ways, over the tiniest offenses.

Reconciliation also means the offender doesn't carry the debt anymore, and the injured one refuses to remind the other of the debt. That's a vulnerable spot. What if it happens again? That is the risk we take. But, remember I said in the first chapter we need a paradigm shift for marriage. Safety in marriage is not about achieving an equilibrium where offenses between spouses are absent. Rather, a revolutionary marriage relishes deeper intimacy in reconciliation. We celebrate restoring communion rather than expecting that we never have problems. That restored communion flows from grace, and that is the safest of all places.

Our culture seems to impose limits on forgiveness. A revolutionary marriage doesn't. A revolutionary marriage thrives through ongoing acts of forgiveness and reconciliation, for the big things and the small. In fact, if we aren't practicing forgiveness and reconciliation in the little things (toilet seats, forgotten dates, lack of attention, etc.), the big things are more likely to occur. So, the best prevention for avoiding big disconnections like affairs and separations is to practice vulnerability, forgiveness, and reconciliation, consistently, in the small things.

The path towards reconciliation for Robert and Gina was not without struggle. There were moments when both doubted they could piece their marriage back together and find safe connection again. After much hard work, they saw light at the end of a long tunnel. Confession, vulnerability, tears, and determination brought them to a point of security again.

RECONNECT

We safely connect in marriage when we reconcile through forgiveness. This can be hard but essential to intimate marriage. It requires both partners to take risks and be vulnerable. What are practical steps for living that out daily?

Purpose

I want to help you work your way through the steps of forgiveness. These steps will help establish a pattern of talking through, accepting, and forgiving offenses in your marriage. This takes practice. I recommend that you keep these steps easily accessible for when you need to discuss future offenses or conflicts.

Plan

Make sure you find the right time, place, and emotional temperature for this activity. If the offense is fresh, make sure you are both calm enough to share and listen. For your first attempt at these steps, choose a very simple issue in your marriage—maybe a disagreement about the toilet seat or meals. These steps work for big and small issues alike.

This exercise requires intense listening and empathy skills. These take practice to grow and master. Give each other grace as you try to better understand the problem and each other. Try to listen without judgment; be willing to accept your spouse's perspective.

SO WHAT'S NEXT?

Practice

1. Listen to your spouse share his or her heart about the problem. This includes both what they experienced and what they felt. If you need help in talking about your feelings, use the Gentle Startup format developed by Dr. John and Julie Gottman.[9]

   "I feel… when… and I need…"

   "I felt ignored when you spent so much time on your phone last night; I need time to talk about my day with you."

   "I felt hurt and embarrassed when you complained about me to your mother. I need you to tell me about problems before complaining to others outside our marriage."

   Summarize what you heard your spouse say. After your summary, make sure you confirm they feel understood by asking, "Do you feel like I understand?"

2. Switch roles. Share your perspective and feelings, using the same format above.

3. Each of you should take turns and share the part of this conflict that was hard for you. What made you most upset? What specifically provoked you in this conflict?

9 John M. Gottman and Julie Schwartz Gottman, *The Science of Couples and Family Therapy—Behind the Scenes at the Love Lab* (New York, W.W. Norton and Company, 2018)

SO WHAT'S NEXT?

Summarize what each shared and switch roles as in steps 1 and 2. Make sure both of your summaries help each other feel understood.

4. Each party should take responsibility for her or his part in the conflict. Be specific and sincere.

5. Apologize. Say what you plan to do differently next time. Just saying you are sorry can sound trite and insincere, but stating your plans for future behavior can make it more genuine.

6. If your attempts to work through this process keep escalating into anger, you may need help from a therapist. Sometimes injuries are too severe and trust too thin to allow you to process these problems calmly and objectively. That's when you should consider a therapist trained to walk you through the hard steps of forgiveness.

Chapter 5

Stable Marriage – From Distance to Commitment

Marcus left. Just moved out with no word about returning. Three months later, Marcus and his wife Stephanie called to see if they might repair their marriage through therapy. There were no big traumas; no affairs, substance abuse, or violence. Marcus said, "We just grew apart." Stephanie agreed, and added, "We're just roommates. I cannot remember our last meaningful conversation."

Their marriage started well. They had great memories of their early years of marriage and the births of their three children. The children are all healthy and successful adults. But once the kids left home, the space between Marcus and Stephanie grew into a vast gulf. They worked long hours, rarely shared meals, and had no mutual hobbies, friends, or interests. Marcus was always on his laptop or watching sports on TV. Stephanie would scroll through Facebook in bed. They often fell asleep in silence.

Marcus told us, "The canyon between us had grown so wide, I didn't think we could bridge it." But, the three months apart ended up sounding a wake-up call. The dramatic absence got their attention. Stephanie said they realized they were "missing something" and they both independently began to long for each other. Though the distance of the past five years led to feelings of doubt, they decided to return. They wanted to bring greater clarity and strength to their marital commitment.

Our culture reflects an insatiable appetite for certainty. We look for fast answers through Google and other searches. We want quick fixes through the newest strategies, self-help books, and medicines. We buy the newest and best technologies to make our lives easier. We want something sure and stable to hold on to.

Yet, we keep coming up disappointed. Like a drug, our gratification hits fast and then fades. We do not persist long term to accomplish our goals or build anything of value. Our "quick fix" mentality seems to place many things on a shaky foundation. We can sustain very few things with quick fixes. We need to struggle over the long term to build or find stability. A persistent stick-to-it attitude is essential for the accomplishment of goals. We must have commitment.

Too often in my work, I see couples and families looking for the magic bullet to fix relationships. I've heard every variation of, "Give me a formula... tell me three steps." In all my years, I have found no shortcuts to success in marriage and family life. If I had, I would have written a bestseller. This book presents no easy answers. In fact, it is the exact opposite. Hard work and taking a long view of marriage are necessary. Commitment to that "long obedience in the same direction" process is essential. Dedication in marriage provides the foundation for deeper connections and intimacy.

We build trust on commitment. And, commitment is the anchor that holds us fast in a storm.

Our family has been a band family for several years. Both of our girls have played instruments through middle and high school; both accomplished exceptional things musically. Our older daughter is studying music (saxophone and keyboards) in college, and our younger daughter played flute in high school. I believe band kiddos are the hardest-working students in any high school. Though our daughters have achieved great things musically, one of the greatest lessons they have learned is the value of commitment. Bands are made up of individual musicians, but great bands hit their peak when members commit to growing their musical skills and to rehearsals as an ensemble. Successful bands take hours of dedication to perform beautiful works of art.

Marriage is no different.

It requires the clear dedication of both partners to make it all work. Husbands and wives must be willing to improve and mature, working together to achieve goals as a couple. If they apply all their energy to self-improvement, the marriage suffers. If they work together with no self-improvement, old problems do not get resolved, gridlock ensues, and conflict eventually breaks up the marriage. Harmonious marriage calls couples to mature and to collaborate.

Commitment Produces Stability

Stability is essential to all intimate relationships. It helps eliminate uncertainty. So what contributes to our sense of security in marriage?

In Chapter 4, I asked you to imagine the mom sitting on the playground observing her child play (as a picture of attachment). Return to that mental scene, but this time notice two moms on the same playground. Their two children have run off to play on the equipment. One mom sits on the bench, watching her child play. She yells occasional encouragement and responds when her child calls. You can see the energy and life between them is friendly, warm, and safe. The second mom sits on another bench. She is absorbed in her smartphone, scrolling her Instagram feed, texting a friend, and playing a game with an online "friend." When her child calls for her attention, this mom doesn't even hear. Sometimes she will respond with, "Just a minute," or "OK, hold on." Eventually, her child stops calling and becomes inactive and bored. The child may even resort to bad behavior to gain extra attention. The patterns of their connections move from unpredictable to frustrated, and eventually to silent.

The contrast between the two mother-child images falls along the continuums of connection/disconnection and stability/instability. The first mom shows a commitment to engagement. The second mom exhibits disengagement. Children quickly get the message that other things are more important.

In my doctoral research, I interviewed several foster parents about their attachment experiences with caregivers (parents, grandparents, etc.) when they were children. We talked about how those early experiences influenced their care of foster children. I wanted to know if they saw a connection between their earliest attachments and their ability to attach to the foster children in their care. I found that some adults remembered early times that their caregivers were both predictable and available. They understood their parents or other caregivers to be dedicated to them. Many of them talked about how parental acceptance and commitment made them feel secure. They knew their families would be there as needed. Those with negative attachment experiences often told stories of unpredictability and rejection. While (or because) their caregivers did not model dedication, the foster parents said they wanted to change that negative experience in their own families; they wanted to offer something better to the foster kids in their care.

James Coan,[10] a researcher at the University of Virginia, found something similar when looking at marriages. He placed women in an fMRI machine to measure their brain's response to the stress of receiving a shock on their foot. One group received no comfort, one group held hands with strangers, and one group held hands with their husbands. Turns out that the human connection from a committed partner was most effective in reducing the stress response. In fact, holding hands with a stranger was no better than going alone. Commitment is an essential feature to moderating stress in a marriage.

10 Coan, James A., Hillary S. Schaefer, and Richard J. Davidson. "Lending a hand: Social regulation of the neural response to threat." *Psychological science* 17.12 (2006): 1032-1039.

Stable marriages require commitment. In Matthew 19 Jesus reminded His audience of Genesis 2:24. A couple leaves their parents and makes a united team. They live out clear and focused loyalties to the marriage. They do not keep one foot with their parents and the other foot in the marriage. They jump in with both feet to become one. That is an image of commitment. Jesus emphasizes, "Since they are no longer two but one, let no one separate them, for God has joined them together." (Matthew 19:6) Jesus knew that commitment was necessary for stability.

Jesus made it clear that the call to marriage is a higher, sacred endeavor that involves a commitment sealed by the Creator. It is much more than a human contract or promise. Sadly, our contemporary culture has reduced marriage to a legal agreement that can be too easily terminated. The call to living out a marriage is a serious endeavor. To be stable, entry into the sacred union of marriage must be done soberly and with a clear commitment to remaining "one." Jesus knew and said that not everyone could accept that hard teaching.

The central issue here is trust. Can I trust that you will be here tomorrow? Can I be sure you will share all of yourself in this relationship? Can I be confident you will concern yourself with my needs? I have seen that the lack of trust, certainty, and stability in our culture is rooted in two problems, disconnection and a lack of dedication. Disconnection is the growing distance, the chasm, between partners. And too many lack clear dedication to marriage relationships. Both spring from deep root systems; both destabilize marriage and community. I want to explore two specific trends that contribute to these problems: technology and cohabitation.

Technology

Technology, social media, and electronic communication have brought a tsunami of destruction to our social shorelines.

Facebook, by far the largest and most pervasive social media giant, promotes its service as connecting people. Just do an internet search for "Chairs are like Facebook" to view their ad promoting the value of social connection that Facebook promises. Those promises are not being fulfilled. The research and headlines tell a very different story about social media. If you search the internet for "Facebook and Relationships," the first 12 links are all negative - "7 Ways Facebook Can Ruin Your Relationship"; "The Best Sign of a Healthy Relationship is No Facebook"; and "Don't Let Social Media Wreck Your Relationship." Though social media, by its very name, promises social connection, it increasingly disconnects people. That form of technology has damaged the way we relate to others, including in dating and marriage.

Up through the 1980s, human communication happened face-to-face, through written notes, or by telephones. Today, texting and instant messages have become the most used forms of communication. In my therapy work, couples often report communicating by text while in the same home or room. They are not talking to each other. And, today's teen-agers tend to break up by texting. According to a recent Pew Research poll, [11] only 47% of teens have broken up face to face. Eighty-five percent of teens say they expect to hear from

11 Lenhart, A., Smith, A., and Anderson, M. "Teens, Technology and Romantic Relationships. Pew Research Center, October 2015

their dating partner at least daily, and over one-third expect to hear from their partner at least every hour. We are becoming overwhelmed with this constant flow of information. And even with these instant communication tools, we feel less connected.

MIT professor Dr. Sherry Turkle has researched the impact of technology on relationships for decades. In the beginning, she was optimistic about the benefits of technology on relationships. But her most recent conclusions have turned negative. In her recent book, *Reclaiming Conversation, The Power of Talk in a Digital Age*, she laments the growing disconnect in our communities and intimate relationships due to the continual stream of electronic communication. She believes the technological stimulation of texting, social media, and instant messaging has numbed us to genuine relationship connection. She worries that we are losing empathy in our relationships because we avoid face-to-face connections. Turkle talks about the Goldilocks effect: "We can't get enough of each other if we can have each other at a digital distance - not too close, not too far, just right. But human relationships are rich, messy, and demanding. When we clean them up with technology, we move from conversation to the efficiency of mere connection. I fear we forget the difference."[12]

Technology offers a protective boundary in relationships. We edit our words, hide behind our devices, and post comments we would never say to a person's face. Technology

---

12 Dr. Sherry Turkle, *Reclaiming Conversation: The Power of Talk in a Digital Age* (New York; Penguin Books, 2016).

limits our ability to empathize, to share in another's feelings. That's because empathy takes time, and technology works too fast. Technology also makes it easy to express our feelings rather than listen to how the other person feels.

In my practice, I see this problem over and over. Marital dissatisfaction often leads a husband or wife to seek a connection with old flames on social media. I've known couples to fight through texting rather than personal conversations. Some have told me they cannot talk to their spouse because they fear what might be said. They are afraid of the conflict, and they would prefer to edit the words of their text messages.

Being human is a deep, complex, and rich experience. But, technology limits our ability to appreciate that richness. In marriage, we often allow technology to come between the beauty of understanding and celebrating the unique qualities and gifts of our partners. We miss looking into our partner's eyes. We miss the pauses, the silent reflection, the stumbling over of words, and touch. The dance of those face-to-face conversations is not always easy. But that exploring, reaching, failing, and trying again is necessary for stabilizing the marriage.

Technology also leaves too much room for assumption. When we practice empathy, assumptions dissipate. And, true intimacy requires the dissolving of assumptions. Remember the mom on the playground? Her interactions with her child were expectant and engaged. She did not hide behind the distractions of her technology or her own interests. In a revolutionary marriage, it is important to place boundaries on technology and create a structure and pattern of face-to-face connections.

Cohabitation

Approximately 70% of women under 30 report cohabiting with a partner. Forty-eight percent of women choose cohabitation as a step before marriage. Since 2000, the marriage rate in the US has dropped from 8.2 to 6.8 per 1000 people. The time couples cohabit prior to marriage has increased from 13 months in 1995 to 22 months in 2010. While cohabiting, 1 in 5 women will become pregnant; only 19% will marry within 6 months of getting pregnant (compared to 32% in 1995). [13]

Studies in this area have confirmed that marriages that start with cohabitation seem to be at greater risk for divorce. What seems logical on the surface, that "test driving" the relationship by living together would increase the odds of a stable relationship, is just not true. To help understand this problem, researchers Scott Stanley (Sliding vs. Deciding blog) and Howard Markman (University of Denver) have identified a concept they call "inertia." That is when people increase their constraints for staying *in* a relationship before they make a mutual dedication *to* the relationship. In other words, just having a shared address and financial commitments creates the inertia that makes it more difficult to end the relationship.

In their research, Stanley and Markman have found that couples with clear intentions to marry do not face the same risks for divorce as cohabiting couples do. Consider the couple that lives together because it will save rent money. Or, a woman who agrees to move in with her boyfriend because

13 Copen CE, Daniels K, Mosher WD. First premarital cohabitation in the United States: 2006–2010 National Survey of Family Growth. National health statistics reports; no 64. Hyattsville, MD: National Center for Health Statistics. 2013.

she hopes it will solidify his commitment to the relationship. A young man invites his girlfriend to move in so he can financially support her as she tries to finish her graduate degree. All these scenarios place other constraints (emotional, financial, etc.) above a clear dedication to the future of the relationship. That is a weak and shaky foundation on which to build a marriage.

Christians have often railed against cohabitation without considering all the factors and dynamics at work in those complex relationships. That often misses the point. If we Christians place a high value on a marriage ceremony as the necessary step before living together, we will often ignore the foundation of dedication and commitment. Even as we want to hear the words, "till death do us part," do we really understand what that commitment means? Do we hear testimonies of couples who live out their dedication in most challenging circumstances? Do we tell the stories of the couple that loved each other as they buried their child? Do we celebrate the marriage that grappled with infidelity and chose to renew and deepen their commitment? Do we invite the testimony of the couple that survived bankruptcy? Too many in churches romanticize the ceremony without giving enough attention to commitment and dedication in the toughest of circumstances.

I have counseled cohabiting couples and those who lived together before marrying. Early in my career I pressed for the goal of marriage. Then I started to see couples living together before marriage modeling a commitment to each other that was deeper and more mature than some couples that started their marriage the traditional way. I saw cohabitating couples caring for partners with serious illnesses. I worked with cohabiting couples that stuck together following an affair. I have witnessed relationships that lacked a marriage license, but lived out beautiful and real forgiveness, grace, and faithfulness. I learned something through those experiences. Of course, the wedding is important, but it is more important to live out dedication that says *I Will Be Here*.

My professional experience has taught me that a wedding ceremony in the church building is not the most critical factor in predicting the stability of a marriage. A couple that has a sober and mature view of dedication has the greatest chance of success. Remember the mom on the playground. Her behavior sent a message to her child, "I am here for you, no matter what." A revolutionary marriage lives out dedication in daily choices. Commitment cannot be shaky. Every day, the revolutionary marriage says, "I am here, I will not leave, no matter what we face. We face it together." A couple that lives that way—even if they have not walked down the aisle—holds the most important component to their relationship, resolute dedication.

Moving towards Connection and Commitment

So how do we deepen trust and stability in our marriages? We nurture a foundational faithfulness that allows us to connect more deeply. Do you remember the castles from Chapter 2? We saw how protecting ourselves can lead to disconnection, but vulnerability leads to safety. Brené Brown says, "True belonging has no bunkers."[14] We need to come out from behind our technology and other bunkers to model loyalty to each other, and to remain together, even when it is hard and we have no clear answers.

Earlier in this chapter, we referenced Genesis 2:24 as a verse that Jesus used to describe essential characteristics of the marital union. "That is why a man leaves his father and mother and is united to his wife, and they become one flesh." The keyword in that verse, offering the direction for creating stability in marriage, is "united." In other Old Testament passages, that word is translated "cling" or "hold tightly." The connotation is clear - loyalties are not divided and there is an unbreakable connection. Nothing comes between the two. In the other places, this Hebrew word for "united" refers to the relationship between God and His people. He suggests that His people should cling to Him - nothing should cause their loyalty to waver; nothing should come between them and God. God designed marriage to model this commitment.

When addressing wives in I Peter 3:1-7, Peter asked them to make their commitments clear by accepting their husband's authority with a quiet and gentle spirit. They were not to hide behind the outward beauty of jewelry and clothing. And, husbands were to be humble by honoring their wives and treating them as equal partners. A husband was not to hide behind his authority and power, but live with his wife in an understanding way. Those were revolutionary ideas in a culture where wives were viewed with not much more honor than slaves.

14 Brené Brown, *Braving the Wilderness: The Quest for True Belonging and the Courage to Stand Alone* (New York; Random House, 2018).

Peter's message focused on devotion. That creates trust. A husband and a wife were to lay aside their individual interests for the sake of the other. The behavior is important. Peter told wives, "… your godly lives will speak to them without any words." (1 Peter 3:1) And, he told husbands, "Treat your wife with understanding… treat her as you should…" (1 Peter 3:7) We model commitment and we find connection when we come together as husband and wife and remain loyal in all circumstances.

A revolutionary marriage must work hard to build trust. The behaviors and messages consistently delivered in marriage need two affirmations, "I am present," and, "I am here." Being "present" means we put aside personal needs to empathize with our spouse. We will live with a standing invitation to engage what is feared, hoped, dreamed, loved, or what happened at the store; to live in a continual openness to connecting. Be responsive. Always. Allow enough space and silence so that trust can take root. Being "here" means that we consistently make time for connection. That creates a space of *belonging* for the couple. That is how to live out commitment. Consistently connect - with no barriers between us. We reserve time and space for our partner.

The goal here is certainty. Certainty of presence. Certainty of belonging. Just as God demonstrates certainty in his love for us, a revolutionary marriage reflects God's certain love.

RECOMMIT

We live out commitment in our behavior. It is experienced daily between a husband and wife. In this chapter we identified the need to be both *present* and *here*. "Present" by connecting and empathizing, "here" by making the time for connection.

Purpose

I designed this activity to help you develop a new habit for your marriage. It is about establishing a consistent meeting so you can better understand each other. We call this meeting the "Report and Review."

That is a time for husbands and wives to take turns sharing something about their day or how they are feeling, and for the other to be understanding. Sometimes the conversation will lead to more lengthy discussions and sometimes will just be an overview of the day.

Plan

Make a commitment to meet together 3-4 times per week for the Report and Review. Take turns sharing and listening to each other. Decide on a consistent place (living room, on the porch, walking in the neighborhood, lying in bed) and time for these conversations. These conversations may only last 20 minutes, but please prepare to talk as long as needed.

SO WHAT'S NEXT?

Practice

1. One partner shares something important or interesting about their day or something they have been thinking about. Don't work too hard to choose the right topic. It does not have to be something significant. Humor can be an important part of these times together.
2. After listening, your spouse should summarize what she or he heard, noting the most important things. Asking questions to better understand can be useful. Consider questions like these:

    "Can you tell me more about...."

    "It sounds like you feel... am I hearing that right?"

    "Do you feel like I understand what you said to me?"

    "You talked about... Is there something more you want to tell me?"
3. Switch roles and repeat steps 1 and 2 above.
4. I recommend that couples do this activity regularly. It may require scheduling on the family calendar each week. Some find it helps to attach "Report and Review" to something they already do. For example, if you clean the kitchen together each evening, sit down for a few minutes after cleaning to talk. If you share breakfast before going to work, take time to talk while you eat. If you fall out of the habit, just start back up and start again.

Chapter 6

Successful Marriage – From Death to Resurrection

Jim loved exercise; he went to the gym every day. And, at 38, he still had the body of a college athlete. But, after 13 years of marriage, his wife, Kellie, was sad and lonely. She took care of their son and two daughters and managed the house and their home, school, and community activities. Jim rarely helped out because he was usually at work or the gym. When he came home, he surfed the internet or slept. By the time Kellie got the kids to bed, she usually found Jim already asleep.

They came to me at Kellie's request. She wanted more time with her husband; she was sick of being lonely. It soon became clear Jim's time at the gym was the main problem. Though they had exercised together early in their marriage, the demands of motherhood pulled Kellie away from that routine. Jim resisted Kellie's requests (and eventual demands) that he cut back on his time at the gym. He could not imagine having less time at the gym or reducing the exercise he felt he needed.

So, Kellie felt abandoned and Jim felt she did not understand him. He heard her needs as nagging. They were losing the marriage over the addictive thrill of exercise.

We Americans have an obsession with achievement. A constant stream of award shows floods our airwaves. We want our 15 minutes of fame. And, we proudly post our trophies, certificates, and accomplishments on Facebook. We keep looking for the next pinnacle of accomplishment. We crave that addictive rush of affirmation. We want more, and we cannot be satisfied unless we can complete a more challenging goal than the last. Once we complete the 5K, we plan a half-marathon; on and on until we compete in ultimate triathlons. But, living for euphoric triumphs will never satisfy us.

We have lost a connection to the value of the ordinary. God did not design our neurological systems for continual exposure to intense highs and lows. We are creatures of the routine, not the continuous buzz of the exceptional.

Many treat marriage as the pinnacle of relationship. "Getting married" means we have arrived. Too many buy the fiction that our partners will fulfill us in some blissful existence. Yet, couples quickly realize (even on their honeymoon) that marriage is not some continual stream of bliss and excitement. Marriage can and will become mundane and even difficult. That's when too many couples turn away from reality to look for the next thrill. Trying to spice things up sexually can lead to pornography, affairs, or even other more extreme and dangerous sexual choices. They might spend large sums of money on recreation and vacations, going into debt. Yet, none of these satisfy, and feelings of emptiness remain.

Although we all love the big joyous moments in marriage, those do not breathe life into marriage. The oxygenating of blood in marriage flows from the small acts of grace and kindness that are common, frequent, and often unnoticed. A husband rubs his wife's feet every night. A wife prepares her husband's coffee every morning. A husband does the dishes or folds the laundry without being asked. The wife reaches for her husband's hand or writes him a note of admiration. These are wonderful stories; they are not done to demand attention, or receive accolades. But they fuel a steady fire; they represent the burning coals of true and steady love. Dazzling fireworks do not sustain marriage, but the home-fire coals will carry couples through many days and nights of adversity.

This chapter focuses on how to develop the lasting and steady love that defines success in marriage. Being married 50 years is a great accomplishment, but it carries little meaning if the couple does not practice grace, unmerited favor. This is the measure of success, because grace breathes life.

I have often struggled with those marriage retreat weekends that seem to offer quick fixes for marriages. Their recommended solutions present often illusory experiences that offer emotional highs but don't resolve the underlying disconnection and relationship decay. They too often feed the myth that excitement and joy are signposts of a successful and vibrant marriage. For example, most retreats suggest the importance of regular date nights. I support that idea, but too often they are superficial acts that cover over a lack of grace and good-will in the marriage. Date nights are nice, but the small and ordinary acts of grace will keep love alive.

The veneer of financial success, great vacations, and well-behaved children can be very thin. It does not help the husband and wife who are celebrating their 25th anniversary, but haven't slept in the same room for 10 years. Wives promote the success of their children, but secretly resent their husband and his work. Husbands earn sales awards and build huge retirement funds, while having no desire to share retirement years with their wives.

Divorce is Death

Divorce marks the failure of many relationships that started with great promise. So how did a couple get there? How did the hopes and dreams for "till death do us part" die? I have seen that a majority of divorces occur after a prolonged terminal illness within the marriage.

As I mentioned in Chapter 1, divorce rates hover at a rate of 40-50%, depending on how you calculate them. Unfortunately, our attitude toward divorce in many churches has been a "just don't do it" approach that has never really addressed the true problem. Christian marriages are ending at rates similar to those who don't profess faith. As Christians, God calls us to live by higher standards than those proposed by our culture. So why are we not seeing better outcomes in Christian marriages?

When Patricia and I were first married, we heard great messages on marriage from several wise professors at the university we attended. One professor asked everyone in our class to raise our hands if we ever thought we could ever get a divorce. The room was filled with newlyweds; I didn't see one hand raised. But, our teacher explained that divorce was a possibility for everyone in that room, and the first step towards preventing it was to face that reality. If we adopted the "just don't do it" mentality toward divorce, we might neglect the hard work of marriage. Without the risk of divorce, we have very little motivation to work toward preventing it. Our marriage changed because of that class. We renewed our commitment to love and honor each other in ways that would never take the other for granted. We would not allow the seed of divorce to be planted between us.

I have found that couples who assume they can't get divorced are sometimes unprepared for the challenges of marriage. When the problems come, and they will come, they often bury their heads in the sand hoping it will just get better. But, that allows the problems between them to grow. Some try to "fix" their partner. That creates cycles of criticism and defensiveness that just escalate until their conflicts sometimes erupt into war. Others disengage from the marriage and find emotional support or fulfillment elsewhere—addictions, work, or emotional and physical affairs.

Divorce is symptomatic of a deeper disease. We need to focus on strategies that address the early stages of affliction in the marriage before the illness becomes terminal. Husbands and wives must do everything possible to prevent an infection of disparagement and distance from taking root in the marriage. Marriages can succeed when we reverse the aging/

death process and find renewal, rebirth, and resurrection of *oneness.*

Patricia and I became intentional about fixing problems early before they festered – no need to let them get bigger. Our focus moved away from trying to fix each other, toward bringing out the best in each other. We knew we were each flawed, but despite our failures, we loved and validated each other's unique strengths. And, we still do; we try each day to die to self-fulfillment in order to serve each other. In marriage, the death of self brings resurrection into new life.

Marriage Models Grace - The Ultimate Success in Marriage.

Let's look at Ephesians 5:21-33, which is probably the most quoted scripture on marriage in the Bible.

"And further, submit to one another out of reverence for Christ. For wives, this means submit to your husbands as to the Lord. For a husband is the head of his wife as Christ is the head of the church. He is the Savior of his body, the church. As the church submits to Christ, so you wives should submit to your husbands in everything. For husbands, this means love your wives, just as Christ loved the church. He gave up his life for her to make her holy and clean, washed by the cleansing of God's word. He did this to present her to himself as a glorious church without a spot or wrinkle or any other blemish. Instead, she will be holy and without fault. In the same way, husbands ought to love their wives as they love their own bodies. For a man who loves his wife actually shows love for himself. No one hates his own body but feeds and cares for it, just as Christ cares for the church. As the Scriptures say, 'A man leaves his father and mother and is joined to his wife, and the two are united into one.' This is a great mystery, but it is an illustration of the way Christ and the church are one. So again I say, each man must love his wife as he loves himself, and the wife must respect her husband." Ephesians 5:21-33

Paul's teaching on marriage starts with mutual submission. That is foundational for understanding all he writes about marriage; it was revolutionary for his time. In that day, wives were often uneducated and treated as property. Husbands held all the authority. But, the *revolutionary* work of Christ in the world turns everything upside down. He overturns the existing power structures, even in marriage. Paul made it clear that submission was required for both a husband and a wife.

Unfortunately, this section of Ephesians has too often been used to promote hierarchy in marriage. To have a revolutionary marriage, we need to consider what Paul said about marriage. He told husbands and wives that submission is necessary for modeling grace. And, the result of submission and modeling grace is unity.

In the English translation of Ephesians 5:22-24, the word "submit" is used twice regarding wives' behavior towards their husbands. But, the Greek word for submit cannot be found in verses 22-24. It is only used in verse 21 and implied in the following verses. So, what Paul seems to say in the instructions for wives is to be careful that their newfound freedom in Christ did not become a stance for asserting power.

The husband submits by loving his wife the way Christ loved the church. Paul called husbands to give up the authority conferred by culture for the sacrificial love in the kingdom of Christ.

These are teachings of submission and grace, not hierarchy. In the New Living Translation, Paul uses 63 words of instruction to wives, but he uses 132 words to instruct men. Why would he need twice as many words to communicate his message to men? My personal interpretation is it appears Paul was trying to adjust cultural patterns of power and patriarchy by overemphasizing to men their need to serve and die to themselves, just as Christ did for the church. Wives did not need as much of a reminder of this because the culture was already driving much of their submission.

And it gets better. Paul wraps up his words to the Ephesians (vs. 31) about marriage with a reference to Genesis, "As the Scriptures say, 'A man leaves his father and mother and is joined to his wife, and the two are united into one.'" That's how Paul presents the idea of unity, or oneness. In fact, Jesus used the same word to talk about his unity with God the Father in his prayer for believers. "I am praying not only for these disciples but also for all who will ever believe in me because of their testimony. My prayer for all of them is that they will be one, just as you and I are one, Father—that just as you are in me and I am in you, so they will be in us, and the world will believe you sent me." (John 17:20-21)

God's grace in joining Himself to His created through Christ, gets modeled in marriage. That's why Paul calls marriage "a great mystery." (Eph. 5:32)

Jesus used "one" in His John 17 prayer as a unity word, a beautiful picture of submission and grace. I believe Paul is saying that a wife's submission is not a response to a husband's authority, as much as an act of living out the oneness that Jesus prayed for in John 17. It is the same for a man. His giving up his strength and authority for his wife results in unity.

Think of it: Two flawed and broken individuals choose to unify and create something greater than themselves. Marriage supersedes the personal identity and desires of both the husband and wife. Through mutual submission, a husband's love for his wife reflects the God image-bearing characteristics of his spouse, just as her respect for him displays the glory of God's character.

Speaking Words of Life—Resurrection

Paul gives us a final thought on living out grace in marriage when he says, "Husbands, love your wives" and "Wives, respect your husbands." I see no hierarchy there, just a man being the man he was created to be, and a woman being the woman God created her to be. Submission and grace. Husbands love and wives respect. There are many ways husbands and wives can show each other respect and love, but I want to choose one that may be the most important.

The most important way we can model love and respect in marriage may be in how we speak to each other. James wrote, "People can tame all kinds of animals, birds, reptiles, and fish, but no one can tame the tongue. It is restless and evil, full of deadly poison. Sometimes it praises… and sometimes it curses." (James 3:7-9) A Proverb echoes that — "The tongue can bring death or life; those who love to talk will reap the consequences." (Proverbs 18:21)

Our spoken words carry the power of life or death. Think of that as it applies to marriage. We have the power to speak life or death to our spouse, family, and to the marriage. The infection starts slowly. In time, the two flawed people find the other's flaws irritate. We notice the small things that we somehow missed or ignored in our courtship. These things become obsessions, and we speak out against them in criticism. So, we say something, you know, something that will "help" him or her.

"You never come home on time to be with me."

"You are always nagging me about putting my clothes away."

"You spend too much time on your phone."

"You spend too much money and you never tell me your plans with shopping."

When passion cools, we discover traits and habits we cannot ignore; we can't let them go. Our spouse meets those "helpful critiques" with a wall of defensiveness and counter-attacks. The conflict escalates. "You always…but, you…" The capacities for listening and empathy retreat behind castle walls for protection. The wounds and scars from the conflict carry lasting damage. They fester into toxic infections. Critical words bring death. They have no place in the revolutionary marriage. People do the best they can; they need grace above all.

Life-giving words heal and soothe. Let these words just flow across your heart and mind: "Gentle words are a tree of life…" (Proverbs 15:4a) "The words of the godly are a life-giving fountain" … (Proverbs 10:11a)." Life-giving words build the safe space we talked about in Chapter 4. Speaking life into your spouse affirms the stability and commitment presented in Chapter 5. The chosen vocation of marriage requires the cultivation of your spouse's true nature, not criticism. The Bible calls Satan the "accuser." When we criticize, we listen to the accuser and speak his accusations right into our spouse's heart. Those words become a scalpel that slices his or her heart, exposing the dark and mysterious places, allowing the infection to set in. But, words of life bring a healing ointment to the infected areas. When our words are gentle and supportive, our spouse feels safe enough to expose his or her weaknesses and failures. Then the couple can talk through the paths forward.

Jim and Kellie eventually found a path away from the cliff in their marriage. Kellie stopped criticizing her husband's passion for exercise. She began to listen to his needs. Jim dropped his defensiveness and started to listen to Kellie's needs. He saw and acknowledged how his lack of availability made her feel abandoned. They pressed through hard conversations. Empathy and understanding opened a door to discussions and plans about a new future. Rather than growing apart, Jim and Kellie learned to honor each other. They discovered how to help each other become whom God created them to be.

So how do we deal with the inevitable conflict that comes from two broken people living in a unified marriage? We become vulnerable, clearly speak our needs in mutual submission, and then learn to meet the needs of our spouse. "Two are better than one" (Eccl 4:9).

How to Have a Resurrection Marriage

Several years ago, Dr. John Gottman researched newlywed couples during the first six years of their marriage. One result focused on what he called "bids." A bid is any attempt from a partner for attention, affection, or affirmation. Spouses respond by in one of three ways, positively "turning toward," rejecting, or ignoring bids. Gottman found that the most satisfied couples, after six years of marriage, responded to bids positively 86% of the time. Couples that later divorced only "turned toward" the other 33% of the time.[15]

We should all ask ourselves every day, "Do I treat my spouse in a way that builds? Do my words strengthen her to serve the purposes that God has for her life? Am I turning towards him in a way that affirms him and his needs?"

What does that look like? I see some very practical steps that can take us toward a successful marriage. To experience renewal and resurrection requires work; remember marriage is a chosen *vocation*. God did not bless you with marriage as a reward for living a good life. Marriage is not a means for you to achieve the pinnacle of human experience. Being single and being married are equal in challenge and value in God's

15 John M. Gottman and Nan Silver, The Seven Principles for Making Marriage Work: A Practical Guide from the Country's Foremost Relationship Expert, (New York, Harmony Books, 2015)

kingdom. Married or single, you have certain responsibilities and expectations in the work of God's kingdom appearing "on earth as in Heaven." If you want a complete view of this topic, look at I Corinthians 7. If you feel called to marriage, be faithful to your spouse, but above all choose marriage as a way to serve the Lord.

Here are more practical ways that you can bring life and speak affirming words to your marriage and spouse

1. Don't criticize your spouse.

   Words of criticism demean and degrade God's creation. When you judge, nag, blame, condemn or engage in other forms of criticism, you place yourself in an arrogant and unauthorized position over your spouse. To do that is to sit in the Lord's seat! That has no place in a Christian marriage.

2. Share your feelings

   Anyone, any spouse, can provide honest feedback about how their behavior affected you, or made you feel. To say, "You disrespected me" is an accusation; "I felt disrespected" is not. And, you never speak with contempt, but always in a spirit of humility and vulnerability. Share your feelings gently. Let the golden rule guide you; speak as you want him or her to speak to you. That almost always means give your spouse the benefit of the doubt. Wouldn't you want that?

3. Share your needs

   This not only requires the vulnerability, but risk and submission. Telling your spouse what you need means you open your heart to rejection but equally give your spouse the opportunity to serve you.

4. Listen empathically - Turn Toward

   Remember, Dr. Gottman called a positive response to bids, "turning toward." We should all practice turning toward our spouses as they share. Empathize, feel what our spouse feels. Try to walk in their shoes. Climb inside what they are feeling until you discover why they feel that way. Don't set out to solve a problem. Empathy is just a place of understanding. It means we can excavate the darker place together.

Conclusion

To choose marriage, to embrace the vocation of submission, is to find a path to new life. Not only does a marriage create new life through childbirth, but each spouse becomes a new creature within the marriage. A successful marriage changes us. We hold the high honor of helping our spouses grow as image-bearing reflections of our Creator God. That is part of being a new creation. That's why we speak words of life to each other.

How does that work?

1. Vulnerability exposes. Therefore, it must be handled with care. This comes from 1) sharing my heart, and 2) listening and holding the heart of my spouse. Both are necessary. Sharing my heart exposes my deepest parts, the things about myself I am even still trying to understand. Listening is a submissive act, meaning I set aside all personal agendas to grasp my spouse's feelings.

2. Empathy is a sacred space. When we empathize, we seek to understand the experience of the other. Jesus' incarnation was the ultimate act of empathy. When we do empathy well we connect our spouse's experience with something within our own identity. That is a sacred space of intimacy.

3. In marriage, we walk the path forward *together*. In this space of understanding and empathy, sometimes what needs to be done next is clear and sometimes it isn't. Many of you know the story of two friends on a long journey together, discussing the dark and difficult place they faced. Sam told his friend Frodo, "…And we shouldn't be here at all, if we'd known more about it before we started…Folk seem to have been just landed in them, usually—their paths were laid that way, as you put it. But I expect they had lots of chances, like us, of turning back, only they didn't…I wonder what sort of tale we've fallen into?"[16]

The point here is not to "fix a problem," but to sit together, walk together, and be together on whatever steps need to be taken. Jesus' command is to "Follow me." Pretty simple, but that decision changes us. The same is true in marriage. The primary act of empathizing together changes each of you. That is the space where both marriage partners are "resurrected" to be a better image-bearer of the Creator God.

16 J.R.R. Tolkien, *The Lord of the Rings Part Two: The Two Towers*, (New York, Random House, 1965).

REVIVE

Speaking words that refresh, renew and revive is essential in marriage. It is the nourishment that sustains us in the droughts of life. It can be easy in the daily chaos of family life to miss out on the opportunities to share simple appreciations.

Purpose

I designed this exercise to accomplish two purposes. First, to identify and speak words of affirmation and validation into our spouse right now. The second is to create a stockpile that you can draw from as you reaffirm your spouse's value.

Plan

You will need to do some pre-work for this activity. Make a list of 5 attributes or values (strong, beautiful, organized, etc.) that you believe describe your spouse. Beside each, write a couple of sentences describing how your spouse displays that descriptor in your marriage (i.e. "He is dependable; if there is a project that needs done he does so quickly," "She is thoughtful. Her planning for family birthdays always considers the needs of everyone involved.").

Make a second list of 5 more attributes and values. This should give you a list of 10 in total. Set this second list aside for use later. Keep it private.

SO WHAT'S NEXT?

Practice

Present your first list of 5 with each other, and share the most recent or most significant experience that revealed that attribute.

Make plans to look for times in the next two weeks that your spouse exhibits the behaviors from your second list. Be sure to tell them in that moment how much you appreciate that quality that you just saw. This should give you a season of a couple weeks of intentional gift-giving through verbal validation. Try to develop the habit of soaking your thoughts and reflections about your spouse in these 10 positive qualities that you have identified. Share your appreciation frequently.

Chapter 7
Marriage That Changes the World

The couples that come to me for therapy are looking for answers. I know what most of them do not, that the change they seek will be difficult. That's because the change *we* create will usually be superficial, short-term, and ineffective; we don't like pain. So, we design "change" that changes nothing. Real change invades, and it hurts; it comes from outside, often through a crisis, a loss, a failure. That kind of change pulls us through a reexamination of our deepest values and beliefs.

Think of how HVAC systems work. They change the temperature in a home in two ways. The first requires adjusting the thermostat. Cooler or warmer. The system kicks on and lowers or raises the temperature. You made a change. But the adjustment will only serve temporarily. Then, you do it all over again. Those adjustments work like the minor tit-for-tat bargains couples or families make to raise or lower the emotional temperature in the home.

But, the second type of change requires a complete gutting of the system. You replace it with a new, more energy-efficient, high-tech unit that should last a couple of decades. That kind of change takes you through an extensive and expensive process to get a system that functions in a whole new way. The HVAC still cools or heats the house, but it does it differently; it will be better for the environment and more efficient and less expensive for you. Some of those marriage adjustments have been addressed in this book:

- Moving beyond improved communication, to risk vulnerability, forgiveness, and reconciliation (Chapter 4)
- Becoming committed to time together, not just time management (Chapter 5)
- More than changing roles in the home, increasing the value we place on each gender (Chapter 3)
- Successful marriage is not only defined by its longevity, but also by its self-sacrifice and deep grace (Chapter 6)

Walking Together

While dating, Patricia and I learned the great value of taking a stroll together in the evenings. Naturally, they have continued (with brief pauses) throughout our marriage. We now walk through a park next to our house. We love our park. With the quiet little creek running through it, the park echoes Psalm 23, "He lets me rest in green meadows; he leads me beside peaceful streams." Some evenings as the sun sets, we watch the moon and stars and follow owls, bats, cardinals, turtles, and the occasional fox.

Those walks have given wondrous value to our marriage. They create a sacred space. I have learned to listen and reflect before responding, and Patricia has learned that our walks are safe for sharing her thoughts, ideas, and feelings. My favorite moments out in the park come after silence, when Patricia shares something she has been reflecting on for days. She softens, her tone changes, and she shows great care with her words. I treasure those moments. Those brief spaces of time reflect the unique nature of our gender differences. Those moments feel holy.

I also notice we consistently walk side-by-side. We seem to match each other's stride, an unspoken, unforced rhythm to our times on the trail. Even on hard days, when the walks are silent, the rhythm of being together can begin the healing between us. Recently, one of us suggested that we turn back early because of the heat and humidity. The response could have easily (and appropriately) offered, "No, you go on home, but I want to get more exercise." But, she or I said, "Sure, let's head back." Submission reflected in the simple act of changing plans for the walk. The accumulation of many small sacrifices creates a sacred space where the needs of the other dwell above your own.

We find safety on our walks as we reflect and reveal. You cannot plan for that. Those moments fall gently as we walk. Revelation is not frequent; it seems to arrive as one of us shares something on our hearts, usually following silence. The words evoke empathy and reflection, opening deeper understanding and intimacy. That comes even when the revelation flows out of a conflict. The silence is larger and our steps seem heavier. But, when God grants an opening, hearts open, and forgiveness finds us in our walk. As revelation arrives through vulnerability, silent reflection can welcome empathy, forgiveness, and reconciliation.

Stability requires consistency. One of the best things about the walks involves regularity and predictability. Most afternoons when we arrive home from work, one of us will invite the other to take a walk. It is one way we still date each other; we still act out the invitation. We usually walk the same path. Our neighbors can predict when they might see us on the trails; they even note missing us on the days we don't walk. Sometimes, we dare to walk a different direction, or we reverse our normal path. In those days, we truly live on the wild side! The sheer predictability of our walks brings something valuable – the continual invitation. We haven't stopped reaching out. We also live out our commitment by keeping a structure. We walk the same paths, in the same park. Though this may seem monotonous or boring, the predictability and commitment live out our stability.

As is true of so much in life, success is more about the journey than the destination. What happens between the first steps of our walks and our return to the house delivers much more than just taking a walk. Every walk is a unique experience. One evening after a rainstorm, our return journey brought us to a bridge covered by several inches of floodwater. Our path home had been cut off. So, we removed our shoes and walked through the muddy waters, risking stepping on snakes or debris. Though scary, we did it together, and it now stands as a great memory (though probably not one we want to repeat). Even challenges can shape the success of our time together. The grace with each other breathes new resurrecting life into our marriage.

Sacred

The sacred nature of marriage contains two essentials - the unique nature of men and women and oneness. God created males and females as equal reflections of His image. Throughout history, the battle of the sexes has provoked mistreatment of both genders towards the other. A revolutionary marriage removes the battle lines. The distinct nature of males and females can and should function in symbiosis. Though different, each gender offers a clear and equal benefit to each other. And the supplementary reflection becomes an increasingly sharper image of the Creator God.

What about oneness, the second component to a sacred marriage? In a revolutionary marriage, to be one requires a death of self. Personal needs, motivations, and dreams take a back seat to the needs, desires, and hopes of the spouse. This mutual submission is a place of humility and peace. Rather than a tug of war between competing desires, oneness opens a vulnerable and holy space of grace. Scorekeeping gets replaced with sacrifice. Paul calls this holy ground between a husband and wife "a mystery." It is the territory of deep intimacy.

This sacredness, or holy ground, gives the space for a revolutionary marriage. These two ideas provide a stark contrast to the cultural (and some church) views on gender and marriage. The kingdom of this world tries to keep men and women at war, and churches often exacerbate the battle by promoting male authority over women.

Our culture often promotes marriage as the apex of relationship achievement. And Christians often celebrate marriage as a higher form of faith. This isn't the way Paul saw it. In I Corinthians 7:38, he says, "So the person who marries his fiancée does well, and the person who doesn't marry does even better." Paul saw marriage and celibacy as equally valid. Both paths lead to self-sacrifice and sacred communion with God. Marriage fulfills this promise of deeper intimacy with God through submissive sacrifice and the death of self while sharing a life with a helpmeet - another image-bearer of the Divine Creator.

We experience holiness when we show honor to each gender as a unique image-bearer of God the Creator. I honor the unique image-bearing gifts of my spouse.

Holiness appears when the self dies to serve the marriage. I sacrifice daily for my spouse to fulfill the larger call to marriage as a vocation.

Safe

Marriage requires safety if husband and wife expect to find deep connections. Safety proceeds from *being known* through vulnerability, forgiveness, and reconciliation. We find safety and trust in marriage with the absence of shame. Remember that moment in the Garden before the serpent arrived? "And they were naked and felt no shame." That is the goal for all marriage. But, it takes work. That is the most intimate relationship in which we can fully be ourselves and feel no shame.

Much like our walks in the park, where we find revelation and reflection, vulnerability builds an essential foundation for safety. We've found that vulnerability is often spontaneous. That sense of safety tends to arrive in the moment. A crying child needs a mom to soothe his scraped knee, not a lecture on the dangers of the playground equipment. Vulnerability and empathy often require silence, and that makes most of us uncomfortable. But silence settles emotions, allows thoughts to organize, and creates a space to be heard. Silence is a signpost for vulnerability. If we hide behind the noise of arguments, defensiveness, and distraction, we will not find safety.

Vulnerability also requires exposure (which could be, depending on the circumstances, emotional, spiritual, intellectual, financial, even physical). We have to take the risk to expose our needs, weaknesses, fears, desires, and dreams. That can be scary, but the empathy of our spouse removes shame. The ideal experiences, exposure, and absence of shame, do not happen consistently, even in the best marriages. It's always a risk; anyone can be neglected or rejected. We all have to risk disappointment, injury, and even disconnection. Unfaithfulness brings the most painful shame in a marriage. Shame of betrayal and rejection. A revolutionary marriage makes the choice to forgive, reconcile, and start the risk of vulnerability all over again. The mess of two broken people can introduce a jagged and difficult process. But consistently experienced with the values of a sacred marriage, we can rebuild intimacy; shame can be obliterated. You may have seen the look in the eyes of an elderly couple as they share glances of affection; they so obviously adore each other more than the day they met decades ago. They live in a place of shameless and safe connection.

Shame is obliterated when, during a spontaneous and unplanned revelation, your spouse responds with empathy and acceptance. I share and I listen.

Shame is obliterated when silence creates a space for vulnerability, grace, forgiveness, and reconciliation. I reconcile.

Stable

Stability is essential to all intimate relationships. The security and trust in the relationship cannot exist if the relationship might not be here tomorrow. As I wrote in Chapter 5, cohabitation typically starts with an unspoken assumption that the relationship is under evaluation. Couples living together outside marriage are often too timid to bring emotional, intellectual, and spiritual boundaries and definitions on their relationship. But, those very details provide an essential structure for an enduring and reliable relationship. If the foundational commitment is missing, the relationship can only be built on flimsy feelings and emotional expressions. That makes the level of dedication to the relationship suspect, and that creates distrust. [Stability needs the commitment constraints of public confession in the marriage ceremony, a financial relationship, and legal ties (marriage license).] Additionally, in recent decades, alliances (marriage and cohabitation) have become more self-focused, making the purpose more about personal growth. These factors have combined to create an unpredictable and unstable state for marital (and other) relationships in our culture.

That cultural milieu means we are connecting less frequently and our relationships are more shallow. Our deepest emotional connections bring less satisfaction. As discussed earlier, technology plays a significant role in the problems of marriage. But, we must press through all the barricades to live out our dedication to our marriages. This creates a structure for intimacy and consistent invitations to connect. We will know more reliable stability and security when we invite our spouses into a relationship and they can know what to expect.

Recommitment is achieved when invitations to connect are both offered and received - it is the dance of dedication. I am present.

Recommitment is achieved when consistent routine provides structure for time together— it is the composition for the musical performance of commitment. I am here.

Successful

Today, many people define success in marriage by how many anniversaries they celebrate. Silver is good, gold is better, and platinum is best. Of course, we should celebrate anniversaries, but longevity is only part of the picture. Many couples live in the same house for decades, but do not appreciate or even like each other. The instituting of marriage between Adam and Eve was not measured solely by endurance.

In this book, I have defined a revolutionary marriage as achieving success in the enduring legacy and example it models to others. The amount of time spent together misses the point. Ephesians 5 suggests that marriage is a billboard for Jesus' relationship with the church. God designed marriage to model grace. Success in marriage reveals the couple's ability to live out that grace in a world that strains or injures human relationships. Challenges in life (health, finances, relationships, etc.) stretch the marriage relationship, sometimes to the point of breaking. Every marriage faces the risk of emotional damage and distance. The only way to manage those challenges is submission and sacrifice. We do what is best for the other. When we exhibit mutual death of self, grace comes into focus. So, death builds the path to new life.

How do others see your marriage? Do your children see you model sacrifice and forgiveness? Does your family know your marriage to be sealed with commitment? Do your neighbors see you treat your spouse with grace and gentleness? When you face challenges, does your commitment waver? Do life's problems drive to disconnection or to reconciliation? Do your children (and neighbors!) hear you threaten to leave? Or would others say you regularly sacrifice for your partner?

The world is dying. But a revolutionary marriage—a union of the sacred, safe, and stable experiences—creates new life. All marriages should know the beauty and power of resurrection. A good marriage brings life and redemption to people, thoughts, and emotions. In my work with divorcing couples, I've always been amazed at the healing and new life that come through the reconciliation of a relationally dead husband and wife. All marriages pass through storms—perhaps illness, occupational failure, depression, infidelity, or even just harsh words. But, grace brings life.

Each case can model marital death or the sweet aroma of sacrifice that models the hope of new life in Christ. A profound mystery rises from these acts of love, and in that mystery the Creator is glorified.

Marriage is successful when there is greater emphasis on the practice and depth of intimacy rather than length of time together. I desire depth by seeking to truly know my spouse.

Marriage is successful when it practices death of self to experience the mystery of resurrection, through grace - resulting in God, the Creator being honored. I die to bring new life.

Revolutionary Marriage Changes the World

I hope this book encourages you to join a revolution in marriage. If you are married, I hope and pray that you can make changes and adjustments to move your marriage towards its sacred roots. If you are unmarried, I hope this book challenges you towards a different and meaningful vocation (your chosen work for God, married or single).

Some readers may conclude this book is not all that revolutionary, that many of the ideas represent a return to more traditional views of marriage. And at some level that is true. But, as voiced in *The Lion King*, we all come to a place where we must remember who we are! A return to traditional values also takes us back to whom God designed us to be. Does your heart remember? So, what does that look like? What should a revolutionary marriage represent and speak to everyone? Here's a summary of what I've presented in this book:

1. Men and women uniquely (in congruent ways) reflect the image of God, the Creator. I propose the revolutionary idea that both genders are extraordinary and valuable. Within marriage, that diversity creates something beautiful.

   Wives, celebrate that your husband was made for you. Husbands, find a way to daily declare with Adam, "At last!" (Genesis 2:23). Both should hold tightly to the idea that God made you as a gift for each other to experience beauty and blessing. Our gender diversity is God's gift. Let's soak in that gift. That will produce a harvest of gratitude.

   But to experience these joys requires work. This is difficult. It seems to be part of the reason Paul mused, "So the person who marries does well, *and the person who doesn't marry does even better.*" (I Cor. 7:38). The work is growing intimacy, and it takes our time and attention. It means choosing to know and be known.

   Our family has panned for gold in the Rocky Mountains. The hard work of chiseling out the raw ore from deep inside the mountain had already been done for us. We worked in the stream slowly washing away finer dust and debris. It took time, but eventually, we saw the tiny flakes of gold sparkling in the sun. In much the same way, seeking and understanding the wealth of nuggets in our spouse takes time, effort, and patience. We have to discover the layers of gold in their hearts and gently wash away the dust and debris to reveal more of that treasure. In revolutionary marriages, couples work to uncover the shiny nuggets that reflect the image of God.

2. Oneness extends beyond the sexual nature of the marriage. It encompasses the *whole* of the couple (physical, emotional, financial, legal, intellectual, and spiritual). To achieve true oneness, the marriage partners must die to self.

But, that can be difficult. Because we are so soaked in messages of sexuality, it can be difficult to understand its true place in a Christian marriage. In his recent book, *Cheap Sex*,[17] *Mark Regnerus* writes, "… there is a retreat from marriage. American Christians still value lifelong, monogamous matrimony. **But many have an aversion to actually doing what it takes to accomplish it.**" (emphasis mine). He spends much of the book making a case that a primary reason for this aversion is the "cheapness of sex."

Many Christian marriages get off track when they give sexual oneness priority over other areas of unity. In a revolutionary marriage, sexual unity serves as a metaphor for integrating all parts of the couple's life. God's design of joining two bodies symbolizes His joining of two lives. When we see that, we come to understand sexual expression in marriage is just a small piece of being one.

---

17 Mark Regnerus, Cheap Sex, The Transformation of Men, Marriage, and Monogamy. (New York, Oxford University Press, 2017).

The most significant path to oneness is dying to yourself. Just as good sex requires sacrifice, a revolutionary marriage requires the hard work of sacrifice. It means giving up my selfish wishes for the higher purpose of making sure I meet the needs of my spouse daily. When both husband and wife do that consistently, unity becomes solid and trust grows deeper.

3. Marriage is a chosen spiritual vocation intended to help husbands and wives model the grace and resurrection offered by Christ's love for the church.

Your marriage is not a prize to be achieved. Marriage is a chosen lifestyle for living out your faith. You model Christ's sacrifice for His church when you submit your life in unity with your spouse and declare your loyalties for each other.

Your marriage can change the world. Like most significant change, it comes in small and even invisible increments—your children hear you speak gently to your wife. Your neighbor sees you helping your spouse in the yard. Your coworkers hear your thankfulness for your spouse.

The kingdom of God seems to advance in small steps. A prisoner becomes a national leader. A prophet proclaims a shepherd boy king. A Messiah is born in a barn. He grows up to teach in small-town synagogues and hillsides rather than the big and prominent venues. Your marriage is the same.

We often underestimate the ripple effect of our small and hidden actions. Winnie the Pooh said, "Sometimes the smallest things take up the most room in your heart." The treasures we store up through small acts with our spouse can carry lasting impact. We may never know what those effects are, but your marriage can change the world by making choices faithfully.

Come, join the revolution.

REVOLVE

My love for astronomy probably started with watching Star Wars as a kid. I saw the universe was so big and filled with so many intriguing mysteries to explore. Even today, looking at our solar system through my telescope is one of my favorite pastimes. I particularly like Jupiter because I can often see the shadow of one of its moons cast on the surface of the planet. I have even seen two shadows cast at the same time.

Jupiter's four large primary moons can be seen consistently through an average telescope—Io, Europa, Ganymede, and Callisto. Three of them share an "orbital resonance." For every orbit that Ganymede makes, Europa makes 2 and Io makes 4. That means from the surface of Jupiter, every seven earth days you can see Ganymede once, Europa twice, and Io four times. Their revolutions are in synchrony, requiring constancy and rhythm.

I see a message for marriage here. The moons revolve not only at an expected pace, but they move with different frequencies. Marriage needs regular expected events that occur at different frequencies, such as activities you do weekly and others you may only do annually.

Purpose

This activity was designed to get you thinking about traditions or activities that you do or could do to provide a "revolutionary" consistency to your marriage. Just as

SO WHAT'S NEXT?

Jupiter's moons appear with regularity, marriages need regular connecting points, like traditions, at different intervals, some frequent and others more sporadic.

Plan

Set a time to plan consistent traditions in your marriage. The planning may require some pre-thought about what things you are already doing.

The goal for this activity seeks a resonance of traditions that provide consistency of connection and purpose for your marriage.

Practice

1. Make a list of current traditions in your marriage. These might include date nights, games, trips/vacations, dinners with friends and family, etc.
2. Make another list of new traditions that you would like to establish.
3. Make three columns. At the top of the first column write "Daily/Weekly", title the middle column "Monthly," and make the last column "Annually."
4. Take items from your two lists (items 1 and 2) and place them in one of the three columns. As you may think of new things, put them in the appropriate column.
5. Highlight the ones that you can perform consistently. Make a commitment to living out these traditions.

SO WHAT'S NEXT?

6. Make plans for assuring these traditions can occur as expected and agree to revisit these at least annually to adjust as needed.

These traditions provide a consistent rhythm. This pulse of your marriage is part of the revolution. Because a revolutionary marriage has a center of focus around which to revolve. It is my hope that the center of your marriage will be Christ.

Author Bio

Mark DeYoung is a Licensed Marriage and Family Therapist with 25 years' experience counseling and helping families and children. He holds a Master's Degree in Marriage and Family Therapy, and PhD in Child Development. He currently provides In-Home counseling services for families in the Fort Worth region of North Texas. His private practice includes the following counseling services: Marriage Therapy, Family Therapy, foster family therapy, adoption work, missionary team consulting, parenting support and coaching. Dr. DeYoung has provided training and organizational consulting in a variety of environments, including churches, missionary teams, non-profits, schools, and child care facilities. He is a Clinical Fellow of the American Association of Marriage and Family Therapists.

Mark has been married to Patricia for 28 years. They have two daughters, Rayna and Rebekah.

Revolutionary Marriage is his first book.